CLEAR CHOICES
FOR CHURCHES

Trends Among
Growing and Declining
Churches of Christ

D1113263

CLEAR CHOICES
FOR CHURCHES
Trends Among
Growing and Declining
Churches of Christ

John W. Ellas

Center for Church Growth
P. O. Box 691006
Houston, Texas 77269-1006

First Edition, 1994

ISBN: 0-9642447-1-3
Library of Congress Catalog Card Number 94-72522

Contents

List of Figures

List of Tables

List of Appendix Tables

Acknowledgments

Joe D. Schubert, while the pulpit minister at the rapidly growing Bammel Road Church of Christ in Houston, had a dream to help other congregations grow. In 1980 the dream became reality when he founded the Center for Church Growth. It has been my privilege for the past nine years to know and work with Joe. As a friend and adviser, he has encouraged me beyond measure.

Thanks to all those who have served over the past fourteen years as members of the board. A special thanks to Robert E. Keith. Bob is a charter board member whose dedication and sacrifices for the Center have gone beyond the second mile.

So many people have graciously helped this ministry. I am very grateful to Ralph and Willene Disch, Jack and Karen Millikan, Bert and Glenda Niccum, Steve and JoAnna Walker, Jere and Kim Woodward, and the entire Campus View Church of Christ.

I am indebted to the numerous congregations that invited the Center for Church Growth for consultations and seminars. Their trust in me is held sacred. My prayer is that the research findings and insights presented in this book will help them in their continued labors to glorify the Father.

My secretary, Carol Warren, has become a true coworker in every aspect of the Center's ministry. Her skills and faithful service have allowed the Center to accomplish more than I ever imagined, including publishing and distributing this book. Also, thanks to all who read part or all of the manuscript and offered valuable critique: Tommy Bush, Ray Fulenwider, Evertt W. Huffard, Judy King, Terry Kiser, Burt Niccum, Pete Petree, Jack Reese, John N. Vaughan, and Flavil Yeakley, Jr.

Finally, there is one person who, for the past twenty-five years, has been my companion, confidant, and inspiration. From the very beginning of our marriage, Cherry has sacrificed so that I could pursue my dreams. Without her love and support, I would not have stepped into the uncertain world of church consulting. In fact, my pilgrimage into full-time ministry was made possible by her faith and sacrifice.

Preface

Clear Choices for Churches was written for the purpose of helping churches establish ministry priorities by introducing members to a broad-ranging study on growing and declining churches. Consequently, several complex subjects that have received book-length treatment elsewhere receive only an introductory treatment and with as little academic jargon as possible. Additional study resources for some topics are listed in the notes.

However, since the conclusions and insights presented are drawn from research using statistical analysis, some study procedures and results do appear in the chapters. I hope this will not discourage readers who do not have a statistical background. Whenever possible, findings for growing and declining churches are given in percentage figures for easy comparisons, and the bulk of the data is presented and explained in the appendices.

One important caveat: a potential danger exists when methodology is discussed separately from theology. It can leave the impression that the author is promoting pragmatism which suggests that, if it works, use it because the end justifies the means. Clearly pragmatism is an unacceptable approach to methodology. In addition, research findings should never become the primary determinant of ministry activities. *Biblical truths (theology) should inform all decisions about church ministry (methodology).* When this balance is firmly in place, research findings can safely help churches in selecting the most productive and God-honoring methods.

Introduction

Conventional wisdom would have us believe that contemporary church growth is really a shifting of the saints. Accordingly, most growth occurs by:

- Locating in a growing community
- Attracting transfers from other churches
- Increasing the rolls by baptizing members' children

Even respected authors like George Barna have drawn similar conclusions. He states, "When numerical growth occurs, it is more likely because churched adults have left one congregation for another."[1]

Now there is some truth in most conventional wisdom. For example, growing churches do receive a larger percentage of membership transfers than declining churches. We will explore this in later chapters. Partial truths, however, are dangerous because they can lead to incomplete conclusions, flawed planning, and wrong actions.

Studies from the "church growth movement" have advanced well beyond conventional wisdom. For the past twenty years, specialists have developed comprehensive and effective ministry models based on extensive case studies of

1

growing and declining churches. (You can find a full description of a valid and reliable model of effective ministry in *Church Growth Through Groups*.[2])

Good news just keeps on coming for those who want to know more about why some churches grow and others decline. An increasing body of social science research is bringing a greater clarity to the complex landscape of ministry. Research findings provide support or call into question case study conclusions and especially conventional wisdom. Consequently, our understanding has taken a great stride forward.

The latest research findings will be discussed in the coming chapters. In addition, a recent study of growing and declining Churches of Christ will form the foundation for conclusions drawn about trends among Churches of Christ. The data was taken from individual church diagnostic services conducted by the Center for Church Growth. It is my prayerful desire that the results of these studies and growth insights will help churches to prioritize their ministry efforts, plan for future growth, implement the plans, and then give God the glory for all numerical and spiritual growth.

Brief History of Church Growth Research

From the 1940s to the early 1970s church growth as an area of investigation held little interest in the American Christian community. Almost all churches regardless of denominational affiliation were riding a wave of growth with no shore in sight. Very few analysts or researchers studied the physics of wave motion or how to catch the best ride. Several social phenomena helped form the wave that produced unilateral church growth. After World War II at least five new developments affected American life: spiritual renewal, a baby boom, affluence, mobility, and newly planted churches.

After the war a religious renewal swept across America. People became aware that life is temporal and it makes little sense without ultimate meaning. We saw a similar but small response during the Persian Gulf War, but the renewal after World War II was widespread and lasted for years.

Soldiers returning home started new families that resulted in the greatest baby boom in history. Recent studies indicate that people in this stage of life are interested in family values and especially religious training for their children.

Also, prosperity and mobility became a normal part of American life. As families moved to the cities in search of good jobs, new churches sprang up to accommodate the new urbanization. Newly planted churches tend to grow faster than older established congregations. New churches draw a larger percentage of new members and they frequently manifest an evangelistic zeal that produces an additional conversion growth.

New religious fervor, new families, new prosperity, and new churches resulted in growth for almost everyone. Churches of Christ experienced their greatest growth during this period along with other churches, but it did not last! The sand was closer than anyone realized, and by the early 1970s the wave had crashed into the shore.

After the crash, observers compared the resulting trend to a "seismic shift" in American religion.[3] As early as 1965, *"mainline" Protestant denominations shifted from growth to decline for the first time in American history*. For the liberal denominations it was the beginning of a huge decline. The United Methodist churches, for example, lost more than two million members in the following two decades. For the first time, leaders were perplexed and reminded that America could go the way of European church decline.

From this juncture, researchers faced the task of explaining the radical shift from growth to decline. To complicate the picture, some conservative groups were still growing while liberal denominations were declining (this trend has continued to the present).

In 1972, Dean M. Kelley offered an explanation for the trends in his book, *Why Conservative Churches Are Growing*. Rather than bringing an end to the search, his work ushered in a period of intense debate. So controversial were his conclusions, that his book has become the watershed event for research, separating a casual interest in church growth from a new and intense effort to identify causes of growth and decline.

Kelley focused on institutional characteristics for his conclusions. He reasoned that growing churches are "strong" rather than "weak." Strong churches are characterized by membership qualities such as high commitment, conformity of lifestyle, missionary zeal, and an absolute belief system that explains the ultimate meaning in life. Weak churches, on the other hand, mirror society's diversity, pluralism, relativism, and individualism. Kelley identified the declining mainline churches as weak and the growing conservative churches as strong.

Analysts agree that "Dean Kelley's *Why Conservative Churches Are Growing* set the stage for research, controversy, and confusion over the sources of church growth and decline among conservative and mainline denominations."[4] Fuel for the great debate, however, did not come from Kelley's thesis alone. It was just a short step for pundits to conclude that "religious and spiritual revival was occurring in the conservative churches, and spiritual decay had overtaken the mainline churches."[5] This type of conjecture was just the catalyst needed to set the debate stage and interest the church researchers.

In 1979, the first collection of research appeared in *Understanding Church Growth and Decline: 1950-1978* (Hoge and Roozen). The entire volume had a tone of reactionary research aimed to discredit Kelley's conclusions as

4

opposed to getting at the reasons for growth and decline. Rather than studies on both growing and declining denominations, it was a limited study of mainline denominational decline. Research can surface and analyze only the areas tested. A study of declining churches could account for only decline—not growth. In addition, social scientists have a bias toward investigating community factors rather than institutional factors. These limitations strongly affected the findings and conclusions.

Overwhelmingly, researchers found that community factors were the strongest predictors of growth or decline. Here is one example: "We conclude that contextual factors alone can explain over half the total variance in denominational growth rates in 1965-75 and a bit less in 1955-65."[6] This means that a church is primarily dependent upon its community context for growth, and what a church believes or does is less important. Such strong conclusions based on limited research fell short of acceptance among conservative researchers and church growth specialists.

Several positive results, from my viewpoint, came from the published research. First, social scientists seriously entered the field of inquiry; second, serious students can see that all research has strengths and weaknesses and no single or collective research project is the final word; third, more comprehensive studies are needed; and fourth, Roozen and Carroll gave us a helpful conceptual framework to categorize the multitude of factors affecting church growth and decline. Their four categories listed below are used to organize the growth factors discussed in the coming chapters:[7]

1. **National contextual factors** are trends and changing conditions in society that affect churches.
2. **National institutional factors** are decisions, policies, and plans of bureaucracies such as denominational agencies or even opinion-setting institutions.

3. **Local contextual factors** are the community conditions surrounding a local congregation, and usually extending out to a reasonable driving distance for members.
4. **Local institutional factors** are the characteristics of the local church. They include items such as leadership, member morale, programs, staffing, finances, and facilities.

In 1993, *Church and Denominational Growth* (Roozen and Hadaway) introduced us to the latest collection of social science research. By the authors' own admission, this new volume was inspired by *Understanding Church Growth and Decline: 1950-1978.* It did, however, take a quantum leap in research quality by avoiding earlier mistakes. They studied both growing and declining denominations, including contextual and institutional factors. And with better studies came some surprising new conclusions.

Studies from the church growth movement are strongly focused on local institutional factors (what a church does). Convictions run high that what a church does is more important in explaining growth or decline than the community setting (local contextual factors). Community conditions are never ignored or discounted; they simply are considered secondary to institutional factors. To the contrary, *Understanding Church Growth and Decline: 1950-1978* left in people's minds the feeling of a cloud of contextual determinism floating overhead. Their conclusion seemed to discount Kelley's thesis handily, minimize the validity of research from the church growth movement, and remove any potential guilt for nongrowing churches and denominations. Their conclusion, unfortunately, left many readers with the empty feeling of a helpless pawn. In other words, churches are at the mercy of society and their communities and there is little anyone can do about it.

Conclusions from the latest collection of research take a 180-degree turn. Study after study discovered that what a church does is a much stronger predictor of growth than the community conditions. Study conclusions ring out like this:

The results . . . indicated several things. Chief among them is that growth is largely in the hands of the congregation.[8]

Churches that want to grow can grow or at least slow their decline. This is the most important finding from among the program variables, and one of the most important findings in this study.[9]

What a contrast from earlier studies! Growth still involves hard work and a great deal of complexity. But the latest findings are hopeful news for those who believe church growth is God's will and that he will give an increase if we faithfully plant and water. My desire is that the research findings from Churches of Christ will also inspire congregations toward hope and action.

Data Sources and Methods

Data for this study was drawn from diagnostic consultation services with individual churches conducted in the past eight years. These services included a comprehensive analysis of local institutional factors and local contextual factors. On the average, a church will spend two to three months collecting data on their community, programs, staffing, facilities, finances, and past ten-year growth patterns. In addition, adult members fill out a ten-page survey giving personal data and their evaluation of almost every facet of their church. The process also includes on-campus observations by a consultant, along with individual and group interviews.

This brief review highlights some strengths and weaknesses in the process, which can be found in all research methods. Most empirical church research uses the survey method. With a single questionnaire sent for a volunteer to fill out, the number of participants in the sample can range in the hundreds. Conscientious social scientists, however, acknowledge the possibility of inaccurate data coming from only one source.[10] This is part of the price for breadth over depth. In the diagnostic process, a congregation's commitment to providing in-depth and accurate data is unequaled in other methods. Such an approach limits the ability to study a large sample, but the data quality outweighs the limitation.

Our sample included thirty-four growing and declining Churches of Christ located in fourteen states and two Canadian provinces. Each sample represents a typical congregation located in an urban or suburban setting, traditional in style, and with no nontypical circumstances such as being dominated by a college campus ministry or a retirement community.

None of the congregations was a new church that is usually characterized by rapid growth for the first ten years. Each congregation represents an established church with the sample having a median age of 46 years. As established congregations, however, each had contextual and institutional conditions that provide some growth potential.

At this juncture it is important to note that the sample was not from a random selection, but was a *convenient sample*.[11] This means that the results from this study can be generalized to churches that reasonably match the sample as described above.

Of the sample, 41% had experienced growth over a ten-year period prior to the data gathering and 59% had registered decline. The average ten-year rate for growing churches was 29% and the average for declining churches was -16%; the median figures were 23% and -13%, respectively.

Growth or decline was measured by changes in the average annual attendance during the Sunday morning worship assembly. Churches of Christ are well above average in keeping accurate adult membership figures along with worship attendance and Sunday school figures. The Sunday morning worship attendance figures, however, are preferred as a more sensitive and accurate indicator of church life.

From the compiled data, 189 variables (continuous or numerical) were evaluated as predictors of growth or decline. A total of 6,771 adult members completed the ten-page survey which produced 75% of the variables studied. The remaining 25% of the variables were hard data items (objective data such as attendance figures) provided by each church office. After the analysis was completed, forty-two variables proved statistically significant as predictors of growth or decline. (Each variable is listed in Appendix A).

In addition, the forty-two variables were divided into three categories for further analysis. The first group of factors represented the ministry activities in churches (called institutional variables or what a church does). The second category was factors that describe church demographics (called congregational characteristics or what a church is). The last group measured community demographics and trends (called contextual variables). Multiple regression analysis was conducted on each group to discover the most significant growth predictors in each category.

Four institutional variables (what a church does) together produced the strongest explanation for growth. In order of significance, they were: (1) the worship assembly's ability to attract new members, (2) adequate staffing, (3) evangelistic effectiveness, and (4) having an adequate number of groups in the church to reach and assimilate new and existing members. (Appendix A presents the forty-two variables divided into three categories, and Appendix B presents the multiple regression results.)

The following chapters cover the most important research findings that relate to church growth and decline. One decisive theme surfaced in almost all data. Chapters 1 and 2 introduce the theme: *growing churches are reaching young adults in the 20-39 age range.* Growing churches also have an age balance between children, young adults, and mature adults. On the other hand, declining congregations are unable to attract and keep young adults, resulting in an age imbalance. This was a critical finding, and it is interrelated to almost all other significant growth variables. Consequently, Chapters 1 and 2 are foundational for understanding the findings and insights presented in the remaining chapters on leadership, worship, membership involvement, outreach, and congregational identity.

Chapter One

Generations in Conflict

In January, 1994, a severe earthquake—6.6 on the Richter scale—wrenched Los Angeles. Surveillance cameras caught on film the turbulent effects of seismic waves. I watched in disbelief as the opposing forces underneath the earth violently shook the walls inside a convenience store. From the altered landscape and rubble of unprepared structures, I could see why this was the most expensive disaster in U.S. history.

A different kind of seismic shift has jolted the American religious scene. Beginning in the mid-sixties and early seventies, *new forces* dramatically reduced the growth rates of conservative churches and sent the liberal denominations into a declining tailspin. This new scenario affected every region and religious tradition.

To understand why a particular congregation is growing or declining often requires knowledge of these new forces. They are the product of *national contextual factors* like historical events, the effects of media and entertainment, and education and employment trends.

Since research shows that what a church does is more important than national or community conditions, why should we worry about national contextual factors? The truth is all factors are interrelated to some degree. Church growth is dependent upon community conditions. These settings change with the constant inflow and outflow of residents. Effective outreach, for example, requires community analysis and biblically acceptable adjustments to serve and evangelize receptive residents. Because these changing urban and suburban communities are extensions of the broader American context, *national contextual factors* are the most important starting place to understand church trends and to design effective ministry. Unfortunately, it is the most neglected area, and neglect has led to numerical decline in churches.

Generation Gulf

To understand how national trends affect the local congregation, churches must first come to grips with the reality of a "generational gulf" created by seismic waves in American culture. There exists not only an incredible difference in the values, perspectives on life, and needs of future church members as compared to present church members, but more importantly a big difference already exists among members in most congregations. This difference is so great that it is best described as a "gulf."[1]

About twenty-five years ago everyone was talking about the "generation gap." I listened and concluded that the whole concept was ridiculous. Anyone could see there was a gap between every parent and child—age, size, education, maturity, interest, etc. I could see no reason to give this serious attention and so I discarded the idea. As time passed, I realized that much more was being conveyed in the idea of a generation gap, as illustrated in Figure 1.

FIGURE 1
Generation Gulf

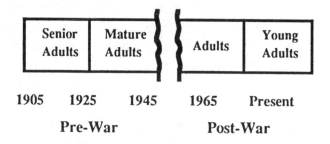

Senior Adults	Mature Adults	Adults	Young Adults

1905   1925   1945   1965   Present

Pre-War   **Post-War**

Persons born from 1905 to 1925 are listed as senior adults, from 1925 to 1945 as mature adults, from 1945 to 1965 as adults, and from 1965 to the present as young adults. Another way of classification is the pre-war and post-war generations. Between these two generations stands a gap or gulf so wide that any magnitude like it has never existed before in American history.[2]

Sociologist Wade Clark Roof in *A Generation of Seekers* divides the generations into cohort groups and concludes that "the end of World War II is like a cultural fault line—the differences [are] greater on either side than between those born in cohort 1 (1926-1935) and cohort 2 (1936-1945), or between those born in cohort 3 (1946-1954) and cohort 4 (1955-1962)."[3]

Division between the pre- and post-war generations is now considered so great that it is *cross-cultural* in nature. This is true even among Christians, but it is especially true when one compares the views and values of pre-war Christians with the post-war unchurched generation. Denver Conservative Baptist Seminary, for example, has decided to train all future American ministers as foreign missionaries assigned to an alien culture.[4] The school realizes that now is the time

13

for adjustments in ministry methods if the church plans on reaching unchurched young adults.

A "seismic wave" of cultural changes in the 1960s and 1970s created a new generation of adults. Because of what they experienced as children and teens, their views, tastes, and values are a gulf apart from their parents. These *two opposing forces* (pre- and post-war generations) have changed the landscape of American religion. Christians may prefer earlier, more simple days, but—in truth—we are left only with serious choices.

Failure by church leadership to address generation gulf issues is a major source of increasing church conflicts. A recent article in the *Houston Chronicle* reports, "Houston-area denominational leaders are alarmed by the spiraling number of ministers being fired by conflict-wracked congregations." The article concludes, "The firings are part of a national trend that reflects the tension of the church's changing role in American society."[5] Ministers are often the casualty of unresolved conflicts, regardless of the sources.

Sources of conflict, however, on a grass-roots level have a repetitive ring. The most frequent tensions develop over worship activities (will it have contemporary elements or be all traditional?), leadership style (closed boardroom control or a participatory style?), small home groups (is this just a fad taking us away from time-honored traditions or is this biblical ministry?), and time management (will traditional Sunday and Wednesday night activities be replaced by other ministries?). These conflict issues are most often generational tensions. Rarely have I encountered real theological conflicts. They do happen, but most conflicts—after the smoke clears—are matters of generational preferences.

Age Wave

This gulf crisis is not going away any time soon; instead it is getting more serious. America has a population of more than 250 million. Adults born between 1946 and 1964 total 76 million baby boomers. Their children add another 70 million to the post-war generation. Together they make up 146 million or 58% of the American population, and the numbers are growing. The pre-war generation is getting smaller while the post-war generation is getting larger and more unchurched.

Princeton Religion Research Center regularly monitors America's religious pulse. For the past five decades Americans were asked, "Did you, yourself, happen to attend church or synagogue in the last seven days?"[6] Attendance has held constant at about 40%, but significant differences exist between age categories, revealing that a larger percentage of the largest population segment (post-war adults) is not in church. (Age group responses are shown in Table 1.1.)

TABLE 1.1[7]
Weekly Church Attendance
by Age Category

Age Category	Yes	No
Under 30	35%	65%
30 - 49	41%	59%
50 and Older	49%	51%

Another study by Wade Clark Roof asked the different age groups if they attended once a week or more when they were in their early twenties. The results confirm an increasing secularity of American adults. (Results are given in Table 1.2.)

15

TABLE 1.2[8]
Weekly Church Attendance
When in Early Twenties

Age Category	Yes
26-33	27%
34-42	29%
43-52	46%
53-62	54%

By looking at American births from 1908 to the present as shown in Figure 2, we can see the magnitude of the growing unchurched population. The pre-war generation averaged between 2.5 and 3 million births annually. Beginning in 1946, the baby boom jumped to averaging 4 million births per year. A drop occurred after the boom in 1965, but by 1988 the rate had climbed back to 3.9 million.

A steep climb in births registered in 1946 also marks the chasm between the pre- and post-war generations. Baby boomers born from 1946 to 1964 account for one-third of our population. Ken Dychtwald, in his book-length analysis of aging America, compares this mass of population to an "Age Wave" moving through society.[9] From the chart on American births it looks like a wave moving from right to left.

This phenomenon compares to a "tidal wave" moving through and dominating society. Dychtwald concludes that "at each stage of their lives, the needs and desires of the baby boomers have become the dominant concerns of American business and popular culture."[10] A high price was paid by businesses and industries that ignored the tidal wave.

FIGURE 2
American Births

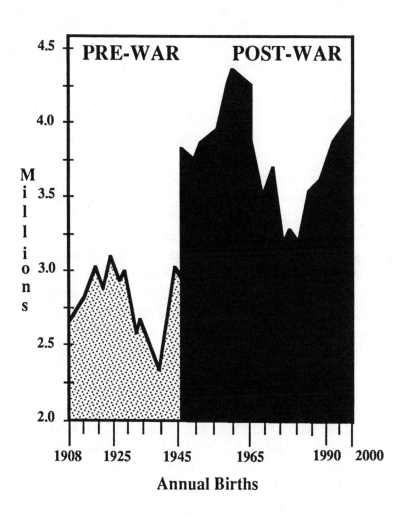

Our present seismic shift in American religion is due to two powerful forces—pre- and post-war generations—with strongly different views and values. Their preferences and tastes in religious expression are often at gulf-size odds. On the one hand, researchers will say, "With a rare degree of unanimity the research of the late 1970s pointed directly to the then-young adult baby boom generation as the major source of the downturn."[11] On the other hand, the same researchers will add, "During the 1960s the 'outside' changed, and churches did not respond to this change in ways conducive to membership growth."[12] The same conditions face churches today. The continuing trend of decline in liberal churches and slow or no growth in conservative churches will worsen if the two generations remain in conflict. Growth depends on bridging the gulf to reach young adults.

Baby boomers may be the dominant force in society, but right now the pre-war generation holds the reigns of power in churches. They have the tenure and yield the financial and decision-making forces. Pre-war adults have built the existing churches, and the church's future is in their hands. If the gulf is ever bridged, it will be because older Christians take the initiative to understand and reach out to the post-war generations.

Churches need to listen again to the Apostle Paul who said, "To the weak I became as weak, that I might win the weak. I have become all things to all men, that I might by all means save some" (I Cor. 9:22). His life and ministry demonstrate the willingness to understand the lost and to build bridges to them. He made sacrifices to understand the unchurched and went to them with an eternal message. Churches have the same challenge to understand the post-war generation and how to minister in a way that we become all things to all people that by all means we might save some.[13]

Paul's message implies a gaining of understanding, a willingness to adapt his approach, and a lot of hard work. A

18

change of methods alone is enough to make many churches balk. Therefore, step one for church members is understanding—why are there major differences between the pre- and post-war generations? Armed with good reasons, Christians can deal with the needed changes. The church, leaders and members, will need valid and clear answers.

Social scientists have spent the past two decades studying and communicating these issues. There is a wealth of secular and Christian books and articles on the subject.[14] I urge church leaders to consider this development as a major priority by studying the issues, teaching church members, and bridging the gulf through meaningful ministry for both pre- and post-war generations.

Reasons and Implications

Why is there a gulf between the generations, and how does that affect ministry today? I want to introduce the issues and encourage readers to investigate further. Conditions are complex and changing so rapidly that church leaders should make the study of American culture and their own community context an ongoing project.

Each person is a product of his or her environment. As children grow up, they develop their values and perspectives on life from experiences with parents, peers, school, radio, television, movies, etc. During the formative years—ten to twenty years of age—each person is deeply affected by his life experiences. Sociologists find that people who have similar childhood experiences share similar values and views of life while those who have had very different childhood experiences view life very differently.[15] *This developmental principle is paramount for understanding the reasons for the generation gulf.*

Children born after World War II have grown up under conditions never before experienced by other generations.

Remember, the key issue is not a person's total life experiences because the pre-war generation has seen it all; it is the childhood experiences that are most important. The post-war generation, as children, has endured changes that have never been experienced before in human history. Childhood experiences are so incredibly different for pre- and post-war adults it has created a gulf between the two in terms of tastes, views, and values in life. And the differences are so great that they generate conflicts in all segments of society including churches.

Several momentous changes have contributed to the gulf. One society-altering change has been mobility and urbanization. Pre-war adults, for the most part, were raised in a stable environment where they experienced extended family. Most older adults can tell about their childhood with the same mom and dad through the years. They remember living close to grandma, granddad, sisters and brothers, aunts and uncles, and all the cousins. Kids didn't need gangs in those days. They were a gang—a good and wholesome kind where children experienced family, belonging, and roots.

Stability characterized America during those years (stable communities, homes, and marriages). At the turn of the century 85% of America lived in rural settings and 15% in urban areas. And those in cities had stable neighborhoods. People took the time to socialize with one another. They knew and trusted their neighbors. One cannot overestimate the value of extended family, neighborhoods, and community to the human spirit. These childhood experiences color the values and needs of this generation, and they are carried throughout life.

Extended family and neighborhoods have almost disappeared for the post-war generation. About one out of five families moves each year. Mobility has removed young adults from their places of birth and their extended families. Even neighborhoods have lost their ability to be a community.

Consequently, most young adults have never experienced the benefits of extended family, belonging, and community. All of this has created a generation with its own particular needs and views of life quite different from those of the pre-war generation.

Mobility is a major contributor to the family breakdown. In earlier years, young couples were surrounded by family. When troubles came, they had a support system they could count on. When marital conflict arose, couples felt the expectations of their support system to work through the problem. Today, very few young married couples have a support system. They lack help at critical junctures in life. Equally devastating is society's value system with low marital expectations—if it does not work, dispose of it and get a new one. A fast-paced, mobile, and change-oriented lifestyle is taking its toll on America's post-war generation.

Considering the different childhood experiences, it is possible to grasp why and how pre- and post-war adults are different. One of the biggest differences is in the area of relational needs. Baby boomers and their children are far more concerned with the need for meaningful relationships than pre-war adults. This makes sense based on their childhood experiences with mobility and the loss of extended family. Everyone needs community in varying degrees. Older adults have had a great deal of those needs met through past extended family experiences. Even mobile young adults raised in the church have had some degree of community experience. However, the problem is acute for the post-war generation and especially the unchurched.

This need sheds some light on trends in ministry. Young adults are attracted to small home groups where the number of participants is low enough so they can have meaningful family-style relationships. They prefer an enthusiastic, warm, and personal atmosphere in the worship assembly rather than the more traditional formalistic style. Music has also drastically changed and so have post-war adults' tastes. Each of these areas is a point of conflict in a congregation due to different preferences based on different childhood experiences. However, change from stable communities to high mobility is one of the greatest contributors to the generation gulf and to the challenges facing the church today.

Dramatic historical events are another major contributor to generational differences. Pre-war adults were raised during a period characterized by pride in America; respect for authority; and loyalty to family, work, and church. In the 1960s an incredible surge of historical events began that jolted the post-war adults into a severe case of cynicism. Young adults have lived through—during their formative years—an unbelievable parade of demoralizing events like the assassinations of John F. Kennedy and Martin Luther King, Jr.; Vietnam; and Watergate. And they just keep coming. Now we have a host of daily television programs—tabloid journalism—showing us the depth of institutional corruption (presidents, senators, cultic preachers, savings and loans, CIA, etc.).

Post-war adults no longer give their allegiance without question to institutions—including churches. Their religious institutional ties are significantly weaker than their parents'. When they move to a new residence, they will visit several churches, and an increasing percentage will join churches of a different tradition from the one they were attending or were raised in. George Gallup, Jr. found that 23% of all Americans have changed faiths or denominations at least once.[16] A study in the Christian Church (Disciples of Christ) discovered that more than 50% of their new members came from a different tradition.[17]

This generation has become a highly mobile group of church shoppers. Their first concern is not doctrinal issues. Instead, they are looking for churches that provide meaningful community, practical Bible teaching, and worship assemblies that are uplifting and inspiring. These and other concerns are so important to them that they are willing to shop around for a church sensitive to their needs.

Churches can reach young adults. To do so, however, will require a major conceptual shift in the way churches approach ministry. The old paradigm viewed people as resources to serve the institution—determine the vacant institutional jobs and plug in the available volunteers. The new paradigm sees the church assessing human needs and continually developing and improving ministry to serve people. Tension can develop here because contemporary ministry requires changes from the familiar and comfortable practices. Pre-war adults have served in ministry that has gone unchanged for decades. Now, along comes a generation wanting something different and they are also unwilling to give their loyalty until it is earned.

The list of cultural forces creating the generation gulf is long. Other important contributors need our attention like the increasing stress on young adults, shifting and hard economic realities, and the debilitating effects of media. I have discussed only two examples (mobility and cynicism) in the hopes of encouraging further study. Some other factors will receive discussion in the related chapters.

Chapter Two

Neglecting a Generation

After reading a few recent articles on the baby boomer generation, several writers left me feeling that the boomers are a scary lot. Several generalizations contribute to their title as the "Me Generation." They are described as individualistic and selfish; they are not committed to the church like their parents; they are a cynical group with low respect for authority; and they volunteer less, give less, and always want more. Boomers are, according to some observers, a bunch of undisciplined takers who want things their way.

If only a part of this caricature is true, who would want this kind of folks in their church? And why would any church reach out to a generation that could be compared to harlots, tax collectors, and other sinners?

First, post-war adults are not nearly as bad as sometimes depicted. True, their views and values are not all ideal, but the real tension producer is their preferences that differ from those of pre-war adults. Second, some words keep coming to mind like, "Those who are well have no need of a physician, but those who are sick; I came not to call the righteous, but sinners" (Mark 2:17).

In some ways the generalizations about the post-war generation are true, but God has given the job of discipling this group to you and me—the existing church. Also, I do not believe that churches can afford the long-term effects of neglecting even one generation. As we consider the research data, our findings offer some clarity to the choices for churches.

Generational Balance

Several years ago I came across a study comparing the percentage of members by age categories in different denominations.[1] After a short look an obvious trend surfaced. Growing denominations have a larger percentage of younger adults than declining groups. On the other hand, declining denominations have a larger percentage of older adults than growing groups.

Even in the early stages of the Center's study, a similar trend appeared for individual congregations that paralleled the denominational trends. After the study was completed, it became very clear that growing and declining churches are different in their age distribution. Growing churches have a membership with a younger average age. Listed in Table 2.1 is the average in each category for growing churches and declining churches.

From the comparison, differences between growing and declining churches are moderately observable. Three of the age categories are statistically significant as predictors of growth: ages 20-29 ($r = .45$), ages 50-64 ($r = -.44$), and ages over 65 ($r = -.36$). This means that growing churches had a larger percentage of members in the 20-29 age range while declining churches had fewer in this range but a larger percentage in the 50-64 and over 65 age ranges. Table A.2 in Appendix A shows the analysis results for each category.

By combining the data into three generational categories, a clearer contrast is observable between the two types of churches. Growing churches have a balance between children, young adults, and mature adults. Declining churches, on the other hand, reflect an imbalance as shown in Table 2.2.

TABLE 2.1

Comparison of Age Distribution

in Growing and Declining Congregations

Age	Growing	Declining
Pre-Teens	23%	16%
Teens	10%	11%
20-29	16%	11%
30-39	18%	16%
40-49	12%	14%
50-64	11%	16%
65 Up	9%	16%

TABLE 2.2

Comparison of Age Distribution

in Three Generational Categories

for Growing and Declining Congregations

Age	Growing	Declining
0-19 (Children)	33%	27%
20-39 (Young Adults)	34%	27%
40 up (Mature Adults)	32%	46%

What causes the imbalance in declining churches? Is it due to internal church decisions, or is it due to factors beyond congregational control? Some researchers have speculated that congregational characteristics are the results of community demographics. For example, some communities have lost their young adults, and churches in these communities cannot expect a balance in age categories or anticipate growth.

In my early years as a church consultant, I had the delightful privilege of working with a church experiencing a whopping 758% decadal growth rate (ten-year period). At the same time, 67% of the members were over 65 years of age. You may have guessed. They were located near a retirement community, and they did a fantastic job of serving the community and even evangelizing senior adults.

Now this may appear as a contradiction to our findings, but a closer look reveals otherwise. Their community consisted primarily of new resident senior adults looking for places of worship and belonging. This church wisely reached out to the available receptive community residents. *This is a key principle for growth within any community setting.*

None of the churches selected in the Center's study had a nontypical community setting. Community demographics in a ten-mile radius of each sample closely reflected the national age distribution as presented in Table 2.3. Each church had a community with an ample population of young adults and children.

From this comparison, community conditions cannot explain the age distribution in churches, nor the growth or decline trends. In fact, *none* of the local contextual factors analyzed in this study proved statistically significant in predicting church growth trends. Community variables receive further discussion in a later chapter. Now we must consider the other possibility—local institutional factors.

TABLE 2.3
Comparison of Age Distribution in U.S.
and Growing/Declining Congregations

Age	Growing	U.S.[2]	Declining
Pre-Teens	23%	18%	16%
Teens	10%	10%	11%
20-29	16%	16%	11%
30-39	18%	17%	16%
40-49	12%	13%	14%
50-65	11%	13%	16%
65 Up	9%	13%	16%

A principal theme of church growth is that most congregations have choices, and what they choose to do can contribute to growth or decline. A major choice is to ignore the receptive population of adults in the community or implement specific strategies to reach them. In a separate study, the Center analyzed new membership trends for twelve congregations. A total of 1,085 new member additions over a five-year period were cataloged by age. *Findings reveal that growth strongly depends upon attracting young adults.* A full 65% of all new members were between the ages of 18 and 39 as shown in Table 2.4, and this percentage does not include the additional children of married couples.

The findings suggest that growing churches were more active in ministering to their own young adult members and in reaching their unchurched neighbors. Declining churches, on the other hand, were more committed to a traditional church culture and style of ministry.

TABLE 2.4
Percentage of New Members
by Age Category

Age	% New Members Received
18-29	34%
30-38	31%
40-49	19%
50-64	11%
65 up	5%

18-29 (34%) and 30-38 (31%) combined: } 65%

Other researchers are drawing similar conclusions. In *Church and Denominational Growth* at least three major research projects pointed out the implications of church demographics. Daniel V. A. Olson, after studying five mainline denominations, found that growing churches are more influenced by contemporary trends than by history and tradition. He agrees with church consultant Lyle Schaller that growing churches show an intense interest in nonmembers as well as members. Schaller considers them "outward-focused" churches. Declining churches concentrate on satisfying long-tenured members by maintaining past practices. Schaller considers them "inward-focused" churches.[3]

Each choice a group makes has consequences. A few churches in our study had kept accurate demographic records over the ten-year period of review. There was not enough data for calculating correlations, but enough information was available to suggest trends. A comparison for declining churches indicated that they were not always imbalanced in their membership. Their communities revealed a balance and the church did too at one time. However, choices that were made affected their membership makeup and their growth trends. A composite of several declining churches to show this trend is given in Table 2.5.

TABLE 2.5
Composite Example of Demographics Shift
in Declining Churches

Age	1980	1990
0 - 19	34%	26%
20 - 39	36%	28%
40 up	30%	46%

Why should a church make the effort for age balance? The need for mature adults has strong scriptural support. Their level of commitment and wisdom is necessary for leadership and instruction. In each time period, older adults have formed the stabilizing foundation for the church. The need for young adults, on the other hand, may not be so obvious.

From the Center's study we discovered that having young adults strongly correlated with a positive atmosphere in a church; an older age imbalance correlated strongly with low morale. In the ten-page survey, members evaluated their congregation's atmosphere and activities. These findings surfaced from correlations between member responses and age categories.

Churches with an age balance felt more of a positive atmosphere among their members that attracted and held newcomers (r = .30). People looked forward to the assemblies (r = .36) and they felt they were warm and friendly to visitors (r = .45). Also, members considered their church accepting of those who differ rather than exhibiting a narrow and critical spirit (r = .53). In Appendix A, findings indicate that each of these characteristics is a strong predictor of growth. Balance is so very important for church life. *Older adults provide the stabilizing foundation and young adults provide the atmosphere for growth.*

A composite picture of the most receptive potential new members emerged from the data. They are primarily in the age category of 20 to 29 (r = .45) followed by 30 to 39 (r = .27). Some are single and some are married. The most receptive group, however, is married couples with two children (r = .45), and their children's ages range between 6 and 11 (r = .40). Most potential new members have been in the community for less than a year (r = .47); others have moved to town in the past five years or less (r = .41).

The two young adult groups diverged in some key areas. Churches will find a greater challenge in reaching twenty-year-olds than those in their thirties. Based on our findings, thirty-year-olds were attracted more by the quality of preaching (r = .41) and excellence in the worship assembly (r = .46) than any other area. The expenditure of time and effort appears greater to attract the 20 to 29 age group. Instead of preaching, they were attracted by a broader range of need-meeting ministries (r = .37) complimented with a warm (r = .45) and accepting (r = .59) atmosphere. All this translates into higher staff ratios (r = .53) and costs. The benefits, however, are well worth the effort. The 20 to 29 age group is a major contributor to positive church morale (r = .30), and they are the most evangelistic (r = .53) group by far.

Church growth, for most congregations, depends on reaching out to these mobile young adults. Each church should carefully study its communities to determine if this data accurately describes its setting. Community demographics could suggest a slightly different approach. Churches should also factor in their own demographic makeup. Starting strategies should build on a church's strengths—not weaknesses. If a church has few young singles, this would not be the best starting point just because it represents a weak area. Instead, a church might discover it has a large population in the 30 to 39 age range. Since churches tend to grow by attracting receptive people like themselves, then the best start would be ministry targeting young adults in their thirties. After a congregation develops a growth momentum and has the financial resources, then is the time to address areas of ministry weaknesses.

Life Cycle Effect

From the composite picture of new members we can identify at least three distinct groups:

1. New members transfer from a same-tradition church.
2. A growing number of potential new members are people looking for a church home and willing to consider a different tradition.
3. A large group of young adults had a childhood religious background, dropped out of church involvement, and are returning to church participation.

While each group has different needs and expectations, a church can reach all three groups through understanding and preparation. Returning dropouts represent an opportune choice for churches. They are receptive, potential new members and, while they are different, they also reveal important insights into all three groups. Studies on adults that dropped out for two years or more and then returned support the idea of receptivity tied to stages in a person's life cycle. George Gallup, Jr. offers this short summary:

> The "life-cycle" effect appears to work this way: people are most likely to leave the church between 18 and 24, as they begin making their own decisions about their lives, but by age 25, they begin returning. Churches and synagogues should be aware that young adults may be interested in returning to church at an earlier age than many religious leaders expect. It's also clear that religion becomes more important for people as they marry and have children.[4]

Robert T. Gribbon in *Developing Faith in Young Adults* sees five stages in the life cycle that he calls "a common journey." These stages are:

1. *Church involvement as a child,* continuing through high school when there was a church-related peer group. Confirmation, adult baptism, or other act of adult membership is common in the years between ages ten and fourteen.
2. *Dropping out* or greatly reduced church attendance beginning between the ages of ten and twenty-seven, most commonly beginning at age eighteen.
3. *A period of noninvolvement,* lasting an average of eight years. Most young adults who are not actively involved with the church continue to be believers, but some are very critical of religious institutions.
4. *A return to church involvement,* at an average age of twenty-six or twenty-seven. The process of return may take several years and is often not a re-affiliation with the same congregation or denomination.

5. Often a *period of very active church involvement* follows
    after a new congregational affiliation is established, which
    sometimes is followed by burnout.[5]

Both Gallup and Gribbon see the trend where young
adults tend to drop out followed by a return after forming
families. The common journey was also studied among
Churches of Christ. Dave Malone researched the trends
among members who dropped out for a period and later
returned to active membership. Similar patterns appeared
where the majority (82%) who left were in their late teens to
mid-twenties. They returned in their mid-twenties to mid-
thirties.[6]

The latest comprehensive study of baby boomer trends
takes a giant step forward in helping churches understand this
generation. Sociologist Wade Clark Roof discovered three
separate boomer subcultures: "Loyalists" are boomers who
have never left church involvement, "returnees" are those
who did drop out and later returned, and "dropouts" are
boomers who have left and not returned.[7]

These subcultures are very different, and yet have some
things in common. Nearly all boomers (96%) had some
degree of religious involvement as children. Most (67%) have
dropped out for at least two years, more than any other
generation in recorded history. And they are not all returning.
About 25% of the total dropouts are following the life cycle
effect. The three groups breakdown like this: loyalists (33%),
returnees (25%), and dropouts (42%).[8]

Reaching these subgroups requires an understanding of
how they are different. We have talked about the differences
and conflicts between pre- and post-war generations. Roof
also sees similar challenges in ministering to the different
types of boomers. He states, "In all these places there are conflicts—latent, if not always manifest—between the loyalist

35

who never left and the returnees who have just come back, and between boomers and an older generation."[9]

I fully agree with Roof. Some loyalists identify with the values and views of pre-war adults. They also can manifest a resentment toward returnees rather than showing a warm welcome to the returning brother. Understanding and compassion must permeate the entire church if we want to reach potential new members.

In summary, churches have choices which are reflected in our study findings. Growing churches are choosing to do the ministry necessary to reach young adults. Congregations need a balance between children, young adults, and mature adults. When a church becomes imbalanced by the absence of young adults, the result is numerical decline. This is a pattern discovered in denominations and individual congregations.

Churches should also take into account such insights as the life cycle effect and receptivity characteristics of young adults in their ministry planning. For churches that choose growth, an obvious strategy is quality ministry for young married couples and youth activities for pre-teens. Keep in mind the need for balance—quality ministry for young and old. We should never neglect any generation.

Chapter Three

Leadership Choices

Anyone recently studying church ministry probably noticed the information explosion. There are more books, cassettes, videos, and seminars than most minds can fully absorb. These can produce in us what Richard Wurman titled his recent book—*Information Anxiety.*

Just imagine, more general information was produced in the past thirty years than in the previous 5,000. And now information doubles every five years![1] The need to stay informed on any subject could create a little anxiety.

Secular success depends on the acquisition and use of knowledge. Wurman writes, "Information is power, a world currency upon which fortunes are made and lost."[2] There is a kernel of truth here for congregations: *the future for church growth depends on accurate information and especially on the willingness to use it.*

Information in the field of church growth is gaining momentum. We have an abundance of resources, but information overload is not yet to the point of creating anxiety. My deepest concern is whether churches will take and use vital insights rather than shelving them only to collect dust.

Some years ago, I attended a popular church growth seminar. As the participants crowded outside for a break, I overheard the conversation of two church leaders reacting to the seminar information about staffing. The first fellow smirked, "Do you really believe all that stuff about ratios?" "You've got to be kidding; I've never heard anything like that before!" was his companion's reply. Such attitudes give me more anxiety than the total knowledge on the "information superhighway." We do have an abundance of information. Our future, however, depends on the willingness of churches to step up and accept the responsibility and the opportunity that knowledge brings.

This chapter is pivotal. Leadership is a major precondition for growth. Most of the suggestions flowing from the research require adequate staffing and appropriate leadership responses. *Here is the pivotal point: congregations lacking the resolve to address areas of staffing and leadership will produce churches ill-prepared to implement other important insights;* so with this caveat let us consider the leadership findings.

Staff Ratios

There is a significant difference in staffing habits of growing and declining churches. In fact, staff-to-membership ratio ($r = .54$) surfaced as one of the four major predictors of growth (see Table B.1 in Appendix B). Growing congregations had an average of one full-time ministry staff person per 125 members; declining churches had one staff person per 200 members. (Because Churches of Christ practice believer's baptism, unbaptized children were not included in the membership figures.) Support staff such as secretaries and custodians were not included in this ratio. These are important positions that enable ministry staff to work effectively, but they were beyond the scope of this study.

Numerous advocates of church growth have worked diligently to educate leaders about ratios. Win Arn is one such advocate. His findings are based on more than twenty years of church consultations. The results of the Center's study closely compare with his and offer support for his staffing ratios. Arn recommends one full-time staff person for every 150 people (eighteen years of age or above) in morning worship.[3] Churches typically have an assembly attendance with 30% or more of pre-teens and teens; this gives a ratio of one ministry staff person for every 212 people in the Sunday morning worship assembly.

Our findings suggest a slightly smaller ratio for growth. Churches of Christ frequently will have similar figures for membership and Sunday morning worship attendance. Membership figures will moderately fluctuate a little higher or lower than worship figures. The findings suggest that one full-time ministry staff is needed for every 125 to 150 people in total assembly attendance. With this adjustment, Arn's suggested staffing ratios are right on target (see Table 3.1).

TABLE 3.1[4]
Staffing Ratios for Growth

Total Assembly Attendance	Full-Time Staff	Part-Time Staff
1 - 150	1	
150 - 200	1	1
200 - 300	2	
300 - 400	2	1
400 - 500	3	
500 - 600	3	1

Rather than ratios, budgets influence staffing decisions more than any other factor. This is ironic because staffing is a precondition for growth and increased giving; growth and giving usually follow adequate staffing rather than the reverse. Seldom do churches have ample funds in advance to hire new staff. In most cases a step of faith is required. When leaders exercise faith and staff produces meaningful ministry, finances tend to follow along with growth.

John C. LaRue, Jr., research director for Christianity Today, Inc., conducted a large-scale study on staffing levels and church budgets. His findings provide insights into the average number of full- and part-time staff according to morning assembly attendance and budget size. These figures are not growth ratios, but represent average staffing conditions. The average church is not growing. His findings, however, show us the current trends and offer a means for a church to make personal comparisons (see Table 3.2).

Elder-to-membership ratio was also tested as a predictor of growth. No significant relationship surfaced between having more elders and growth. A strong correlation would have implied that, if a 500-member church had seven elders, its probability for growth would increase by having twenty elders. Elders spend much of their time in decision making. Studies in group dynamics reveal that the group decision making works best with five to seven people. After that, the process begins to break down. By the time a group has fifteen to twenty decision makers, it is unworkable without special circumstances to involve fewer elders at any given time.

TABLE 3.2[5]
Study Findings for Average Staffing Ratios

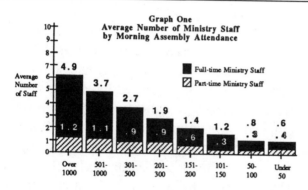

Graph One
Average Number of Ministry Staff
by Morning Assembly Attendance

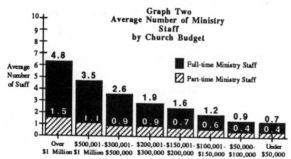

Graph Two
Average Number of Ministry
Staff
by Church Budget

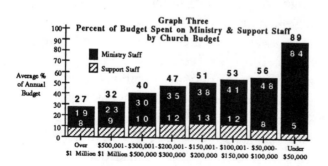

Graph Three
Percent of Budget Spent on Ministry & Support Staff
by Church Budget

Staff or Consequences

With so many interrelated factors, could staffing be that significant? Just how important is it compared to other issues? To answer these questions, multiple regression analysis was applied to the local institutional variables to help us identify which factors are the strongest predictors of growth. Four institutional variables (what a church does) surfaced as significant predictors, and the staff-to-membership ratio was second in predictive efficacy. (Appendix B further explains multiple regression analysis and shows the study results.)

In short, staffing should top the list in church planning. Adequate staffing correlates strongly not only with growth, but also with most of the vital aspects of church life. Well-staffed churches attract a higher percentage of new members, and members are willing to drive further to attend services. These congregations express greater satisfaction with their worship assembly and the preaching than declining churches. They feel they are warm and friendly to one another and to their visitors. Inadequately staffed churches fall short in these areas and tend to neglect outreach while better-staffed churches are also evangelistic. Growing congregations are the providers of quality ministries that attract young adults 20-29 years of age. A good staff-to-membership ratio allows a church to train volunteers and provide excellence in service. Each of these areas is a predictor of growth and significantly correlates to staffing (see Table 3.3).

Churches face a variety of conditions that can prevent numerical increase. These conditions are called "growth barriers." The lack of adequate parking or ample auditorium seating is a very tangible barrier. On the other hand, less obvious conditions develop such as inadequate staffing.

As smaller churches increase in size, the first major growth obstacle is the "200 barrier." Eighty-five percent of

Churches of Christ are under 200 in their Sunday morning assembly attendance. Any congregation wanting to move beyond a small (less than 100) or middle-size (100-250) church must overcome this barrier to become a large church (more than 250).

TABLE 3.3
Relationships Between Staff-to-Membership Ratio and Other Variables

Variables	Pearson's r
Visitors Feel Church is Warm and Friendly	.56
Age 20-29	.53
Church is Warm and Friendly	.50
Baptisms-to-Membership Ratio	.49
Baptism of Unchurched	.46
Groups-to-Membership Ratio	.44
Satisfied with Morning Worship Assembly	.44
% of Annual Membership Gains	.41
Church Accepts Others vs. Narrow and Critical	.38
Drives 10 - 15 Miles to Church	.38
Preaching Attracts New Members	.32

Growing beyond approximately 200 in Sunday morning attendance requires significant changes in the way a church operates. These changes are so critical for success that they constitute a formidable set of obstacles to growth. These obstacles are often hidden to the average member. A vague sense of their presence may exist for some members, but they are invisible as a collective force, working together, holding a church back from growing. To make conditions worse, some members are very resistant to implementing any of the required changes necessary for growth.

The 200 barrier is the most documented problem in church growth studies. After years of evaluating congregations, I have observed, like other consultants, at least seven characteristics present in this condition and the top obstacle relates to staff ratios:[6]

- One minister
- One Sunday morning assembly
- One fellowship formation
- Facility crowding
- Small-church attitudes
- Inadequate member involvement
- Attendance between 150-250

A staffing barrier first appears for churches with about 150 in Sunday morning attendance. If a church increases attendance into the 200 range without increasing staff, it discovers a major obstacle. Observations indicate that one energetic preacher and a small core of active members can move a church to about 200. At this point, the preacher and core members have saturated work loads. Multiple staffing becomes necessary at this juncture for a congregation to move beyond the 200 barrier.

In the 50s and 60s, it was not uncommon to visit churches with 300 to 500 in assembly attendance with only one full-time paid staff—the preacher. Occasionally, one still can be found, but this situation is getting rare. Members' life circumstances have dramatically changed, requiring a different scenario in a staff-to-member ratio. For example, lives are more complicated, more stressed, and more time pressured than ever before. Members simply do not have the volunteer time compared to thirty years ago. This requires churches to hire more staff to effectively handle the changing conditions. Today, if a church ignores these factors, it is almost guaranteed to plateau and even decline.

Also, we are all part of a "consumer society" looking at life through a pair of consumer glasses. I keep trying to find someone who is *not* a consumer, but without any luck. As consumers, we are wanting more and better services from our government. . . from our businesses. . . from our schools. . . and, yes, from our churches. Consumers have less time and want better services, which means that adequate staffing is essential for expanding ministry and generating growth.

Large churches are equally affected by staffing ratios. Just because a church of 1,000 in attendance employs multiple staff, it is not exempt from facing this growth barrier. In fact, large churches are some of the worst offenders of correct staffing. This results in overworked and overstressed staff members who are candidates for burnout. Also, large churches should recognize that staff serving 800 or more must function differently from those in small churches.[7]

In all size churches, staff should not do the work for members. Rather, staff is necessary to train members for ministry as clearly taught in Ephesians 4:11-12. Staff responsibilities include modeling ministry (they do the work) and then training other members to do the same. Getting past 200 and keeping a large church healthy ultimately depends on how many and how well the members serve. One preacher and a few core workers are fine up to 200. After that, a high percentage of active members is required for success. Now, we have a clear connection between multiple staff and an active membership. It requires staff to oversee the various ministries, motivate and train members for involvement, and offer quality service. It should not come as a surprise that growing churches have a better staff-to-member ratio than declining churches.

One final warning: most members and church leaders are not aware of understaffing consequences. Remembering the good old days gives confidence that investing in additional staff is not necessary. Even under a severe staff shortage, I have discovered members evaluating their church as over-staffed. Information and education are way past due!

Attitudes Toward Leadership

A rewarding experience that comes with church consulting is developing acquaintances and friendships with numerous staff members. Often our paths cross again and I will ask the usual, "How are things going?" Responses run the gamut from "great" or "not so good" to complete details on the church's progress. Occasionally, I will experience gut-wrenching responses like "Hey, I'm just trying to stay out of the way" or "I'm doing my own thing and the other staff are doing theirs."

At first glance these responses may seem harmless enough, but the application of the research findings not only requires adequate staffing but also appropriate leadership responses. Leadership attitudes and actions, especially those of the pulpit minister, have a critical impact on churches. The above responses reveal an avoidance of leadership responsibilities.

Our study found a clear difference in the way preachers in growing churches viewed their job responsibilities as compared to preachers in declining congregations. Each group prioritized their most important work responsibilities from a list of thirteen major work-related tasks. Preachers of growing churches considered leadership as a top responsibility while preachers in declining churches did not consider leadership as an important task. The prioritized list of averaged responses for both groups is shown in Table 3.4.

Staff actions flow from attitudes. Church growth specialists have long stressed that the most important vital sign of a healthy church is a pulpit minister with vision and faith and whose dynamic leadership is used to catalyze the congregation into action for growth. Such efforts can only come after ministers first accept leadership responsibilities.

TABLE 3.4
Prioritized List of Preacher's Job Responsibilities

Preachers in Growing Churches	Preachers in Declining Churches
1. Preaching	1. Preaching
2. Evangelism	2. Motivation and Inspiration
3. *Providing Leadership*	3. Evangelism
4. Teaching	4. Creating an Atmosphere for Growth
	7. *Providing Leadership*

Another disturbing attitude surfaced. When elders and members prioritized the preacher's job responsibilities, both ranked leadership even lower than the average response given by preachers in declining churches. Providing leadership dropped to eighth and ninth place for both growing and declining churches. *In other words, not enough elders and members recognize that providing leadership is a significant role for the pulpit minister* (see Table 3.5).

This dilemma creates tension for elders, members, and especially preachers. Staff may sense their responsibility to provide leadership, but their efforts are frequently met with subtle rebuffs and even overt resistance. Some ministers have concluded that it is best just to stay out of the way. When this attitude develops, churches are severely handicapped for growth. It is *better* for staff to exercise leadership regardless of how others view the issues, but it is *best* when the entire church supports staff efforts.

47

TABLE 3.5

Prioritized List of Job Responsibilities for Preachers

Preachers in Growing Churches	Elders	Members
1. Preaching	1. Preaching	1. Preaching
2. Evangelism	2. Evangelism	2. Teaching
3. *Providing Leadership*	3. Teaching	3. Counseling
	9. *Providing Leadership*	8. *Providing Leadership*

I believe that part of the problem is a misunderstanding of leadership. Authority and leadership are often equated when in fact they are not the same. Consequently, when members posit authority with the eldership, then the only real leaders are elders. This view reduces the leadership base of a church and cripples the church's potential for numerical and spiritual growth.

From a practical standpoint, church leadership is exercised through personal example, initiating actions, and communication that influences and encourages members to fulfill God's purposes. This understanding broadens the definition of leadership beyond an office. It is an "influencing power" for God's glory. Obviously, the church needs numerous members exercising leadership responsibilities.

Pulpit ministers have a major God-given responsibility to provide leadership. God has ordained the ministry of preaching, and the single greatest avenue of influencing power in the church is through the pulpit. Churches are only shooting themselves in the foot by efforts to reduce the leadership role of the pulpit minister. Movement toward growth begins with communication, and the pulpit is consistently the most effective channel of communication. This should bring some insight to our findings on preachers in the growing and declining churches. Preachers in growing churches accept and exercise responsibility regardless of others' views. On the other hand, when the leadership and growth initiative of the pulpit minister are extinguished, the church is almost guaranteed to decline.

Actions for Leaders

Growing churches have attitudes and actions distinctly different from declining congregations. Members of growing churches believe in their future and see their potential for growth (r = .36). They view their church as well-organized (r = .33) and goal-oriented (r = .30). Each of these characteristics represents a significant area of leadership responsibility.

Sociologist C. Kirk Hadaway conducted a remarkable study on churches that broke out of an extended nongrowth pattern.[8] His sample was drawn from Southern Baptist churches that were plateaued for five years from 1978 to 1983. About half of his sample grew the next five years by 5% or more while the other half remained plateaued. By comparing the two groups, he discovered key growth principles for changing a nongrowing congregation into a growing church.

Spiritual Renewal

Occasionally we need research findings to remind us of what we already know. It should not come as a surprise to learn that studies indicate that spiritual renewal is a vital condition for church growth. Hadaway found that the breakout churches had a greater emphasis on spiritual growth and prayer.[9] Congregations are realizing that prayer and other spiritual disciplines serve as a significant catalyst for congregational change and divine blessings. Members must change to effective planting and watering, and prayerfully remember that it is God who gives the increase.

Church leaders may know the latest methods, but change of any kind is rejected by some members. Certainly change for change's sake should not be a part of anyone's agenda. However, if a congregation is plateaued or declining, some type of change is the only hope. In fact, Hadaway's study reveals that growth correlates strongly with church members' willingness to accept change.[10] Growing churches can handle change while declining churches are resistant to change.

What motivation or force can free people from a preference for the same old comfortable conditions even though those same conditions are killing the body? Leaders, on their own, are powerless. God is the only source able to free us from our self-centered comfort zones and self-willed preferences. Members simply cannot approach God in prayer on a regular basis without being changed and willing to accept changes that please Him. Prayer renewal in churches is the means God uses to prepare a church for change and growth.

Leaders will most likely find the membership receptive to an emphasis on spiritual renewal. Each church in our study received an on-campus visit and during this time a cross-section interview was held with 20 to 25 members who were selected for their ability to represent the whole congregation. During the interview they identified and prioritized the concerns they had for their congregation. Combined results of all samples reveal the top four concerns members expressed:

1.   Members want a greater *spiritual emphasis* in programs such as the Bible class and small home groups.
2.   They would like to see the *educational program* improved.

3. Members feel the need for better *internal communications* between leaders and the congregation.
4. Members want a greater emphasis on *outreach and evangelism.*

A desire for a greater spiritual emphasis topped the members' wish list. This should provide encouragement for leaders to consider intentional strategies that can help members improve their spiritual disciplines such as prayer, Bible study, and service. Genuine spiritual renewal in a church, however, is only likely if it begins with the leadership. They should set the example. And their reward is most often a spiritually vibrant congregation willing to devote themselves to the church's mission and vision.

Vision

From my observation, another major problem found in churches today, regardless of size, is the eventual loss of vision which leads to institutionalism. Times have changed dramatically and so have the ways effective ministry is conducted. Far too often churches make no adjustments along the way to keep ministry productive. Vision can motivate leaders to seek the best methods. Lack of vision produces churches doing the same things the same way with little concern for results.

In contrast, new churches usually begin with a sense of mission (what God wants accomplished as revealed in his Word) and vision (how to accomplish God's will in the local context and how the end product will look). New churches with vision seek the best methods; for a new church it is a necessity for survival. And this aggressive approach usually brings growth for the first ten to fifteen years.

Then, as a church ages, it tends to no longer develop new methods. With the appearance of a comfortable building and ample Sunday attendance, an aggressive approach disappears. The end result is repetition of the same things the same way, giving the same result—no growth.

Institutionalism firmly sets in when there is no energizing vision for change and growth. Ministry activities become routine and repetitious as if they were the organization's end purpose rather than the means to accomplish the end. Consequently, the mission to make disciples and the ministry of reconciliation receives only lip service. Serious efforts to measure ministry results and make necessary adjustments are nonexistent.

Numerous symptoms in a congregation can surface when institutionalism fully develops. After years of no progress in spiritual and numerical growth, members may experience low morale. This is a feeling of low expectations and little hope for the church's future. The church's atmosphere lacks energy and enthusiasm necessary for ministry motivation. And if a group stays this way long enough, members assume this is natural, even to the point of resisting renewal or any attempt for change.

Another indicator or symptom is internal conflicts. Of course, conflicts arise apart from institutionalism, but when a church has no compelling vision to occupy members' time and attention, internal conflicts frequently result. Rather than looking critically inward, members need an inspiring vision to help them look outward to God and his purposes. Hadaway discovered that breakout churches reported a "renewed vision for growth" and a strong "desire to grow."[11]

To break out of institutionalism, or prevent it, each Christian generation should spend time rediscovering a clear understanding of the church's mission as given by God. A renewed awareness of mission based on Scripture can serve as a catalyst for leaders to dream new possibilities even for old churches. This leads to new vision, new hope, new energy, and new planning.

Planning

Planning is the process that separates proactive leadership from reactive leadership. Healthy churches have leaders who invest time wisely in the planning process while unhealthy churches get stuck on problem solving. Every congregation will have problems to solve, but reactive responses alone lack the motivating force to move churches beyond the status quo.

Growth planning develops strategies for moving a church from point A to point B. This means that leaders first understand point A, then point B, and everything in between. Consequently, homework is a never-ending responsibility for effective leadership. This involves reading, attending training seminars, and visiting growing churches. Accurate knowledge is required for a good analysis of one's own local setting, and some churches are willing to use outside resources for analysis help. Based on homework, leaders can then complete an analysis of the local church that will surface the obstacles needing attention. Therefore, planning involves knowing the local setting through analysis (point A), having a vision of what the church can become (point B), and determining the ministry improvements and changes to get there (everything in between).

Goals

From planning come measurable goals. Goals demonstrate a serious commitment to go about the Father's business. Here are the ways leaders make tangible their proactive leadership, a commitment to mission and vision, and a willingness to confront institutionalism. No more lip service —goals are the means to make a tangible difference.

Churches take "quantum leaps" with goal setting. Each goal is really a statement of faith. It states what the members believe God can accomplish through their efforts. Based on Scripture and personal experience, I believe you would agree that God honors faith by giving the increase. Hadaway's study supports this premise. His results show "quite clearly that breakout churches evaluate their ministries and direction, they make plans for growth, they set visible, realistic goals for growth, and they reach their goals through faith and action."[12]

So what holds back so many churches from setting goals? One reason is the fear of failure. What a big misunderstanding! Goals do not make us successes or failures. They just point the way for progress. If a church overshoots the goal—great—give God the glory. If a church undershoots the goal—no problem—measure the progress and give God the glory. Either way there is progress. We have intentionally planted and watered and given God thanks for his increase.

Open Leadership

Leaders will need to understand one other critically important ingredient for successful planning and goal setting. The old leadership style of making closed boardroom-style decisions no longer works with well-informed and highly educated members. There was a time when decisions made at the top, without involving members, were given to the church with little objection or resistance. Today, members want some input into major issues affecting their church life. "Participatory-style leadership" is a key ingredient for today's growing church.

A participatory style of leading does not mean an abdication of strong proactive leadership nor democratic decision-making. Churches cannot function well with a pure democracy; the larger the church, the more it depends upon strong leadership. Strong leadership requires a balance, however, with a sensitivity to their well-informed members. Leaders cannot successfully lead where members are not

54

prepared to follow. Therefore, when major changes are needed that affect a large percentage of the members, effective two-way communication is required.

Planned time must be spent in settings like large gatherings or small groups discussing plans and options. Such meetings are not decision-making times, but periods of two-way communication between members and leaders. These activities allow leaders to share their vision and gain accurate feedback as to where the members are on key issues. It takes careful planning, time, and work, but the results are worth the effort.

Chapter Four

Worship Choices

"**P**rogress will enhance the quality of our lifestyles" was once a byword of the American Dream. People were led to believe, for example, that modern technology would shorten the forty-hour work week and give everyone more leisure time. Well, conditions did not turn out as planned. People are now working longer hours and living more complicated lives than a decade ago. Even churches are feeling the squeeze. Members have less discretionary time, creating a serious volunteer crunch in congregations. Families and churches are forced to use time management where commitments are prioritized to prevent a person from sinking into a sea of trivial activities.

Americans have cultivated a taste for timesavers, short-cuts, and bottom-line items. "What are the *top priorities* for success?" "What is the *most important* principle for a happy marriage?" "What is the *number one* factor in growing churches?" When it comes to family, work, and faith, people do not have time to play games like Trivial Pursuit. In this study, efforts were made to discover the most significant correlates of church growth. And now we come to the number one variable that predicted growth in the Center's findings.

Number One

In a multivariate context, regression analysis surfaces the strongest variables in the group. Four of all the institutional variables studied provided the strongest predictive power for growth. The significant institutional variables are listed in Appendix A, and the regression results are in Appendix B.

The worship assembly's ability to attract new members was the number one growth factor. This variable was drawn from a membership survey question that asked, "What one characteristic attracted you most to come to this congregation?" Eleven different items were available for selection. Growing churches had a significantly higher percentage of members designating the worship assembly as the number one attracting factor than did declining churches.

This variable should not be confused with the variables where members evaluate the worship assembly. They measure very different things. Eight questions in the membership survey allowed people to evaluate every facet of the assembly. Six of the eight questions proved statistically significant as predictors of growth when considered individually (see Table 4.1). In fact, the average score on every question is higher for growing churches. Members of growing congregations are more satisfied with every aspect of their worship assembly than the members in declining churches.

TABLE 4.1

Members' Evaluation of the Worship Assembly

Variables	Pearson's r
1. Visitors Feel Church is Warm and Friendly	.37
2. Look Forward to Morning Worship Assembly	.34
3. Satisfied with Morning Worship Assembly	.34
4. Preaching Attracts New Members	.34
5. Church is Warm and Friendly	.33
6. Satisfied with Singing	.30

The worship assembly's ability to attract new members is different from members' general evaluation and satisfaction level. When consulting with churches, I often find members satisfied with their assembly, yet the worship will lack the qualities to attract new members. From considering the difference between the pre- and post-war generations, this situation is understandable. A large percentage of the satisfaction measurements includes pre-war adults with their preferences in worship style. As discussed in Chapter 2, most new members come from the post-war generation and they have a different taste in worship style. Another way to state the number one growth predictor is the worship assembly's ability to attract new members between the ages of 20 and 39.

Churches are faced with the challenge of keeping existing members satisfied and reaching new members. These two areas frequently become a point of conflict. Therefore, the importance and impact of each should be weighed and given the appropriate emphasis. Members' evaluation and satisfaction with the assembly are predictors of growth. However, in a multivariate context, they lose out to other more significant variables. The most powerful predictor of growth is the assembly's ability to attract new members between the ages of 20 and 39.

Growth Climate

Climate has little to do with humidity and room temperature; it has everything to do with the spirit of the church best experienced during the Sunday morning activities. A church's atmosphere will fall at different points on a group of continuums as formal or relaxed, somber or joyful, reserved or friendly, quiet or noisy, and meditative or celebrative. Each end of the continuums represents a different preference for the ethos of worship. It is not that one style is right and the other is wrong; both are a matter of taste. The unfortunate reality is that only one side consistently produces a growth climate.

Worship styles are best experienced rather than explained. There are excellent workshops and resources[1] that go well beyond what space will allow here. This discussion is limited to the findings and implications from the study. Each variable discussed is related to the worship assembly climate and each factor significantly correlates both to growth and to young adults 20 to 39 years of age as shown in Table 4.2.

Exciting

Participants in the study were asked to evaluate their congregation by responding to nine continuums. Each had a pair of opposite words like active or inactive and exciting or dull. Growing churches evaluated their congregation more exciting than declining churches. An exciting atmosphere correlated strongly with growth ($r = .47$) and young adults ($r = .44$).

TABLE 4.2

Measurements of Growth Climate

Variables	Correlation with Growth	Correlation with Young Adults
1. Church Accepts Others vs. Narrow and Critical	.50	.53
2. Church is Exciting vs. Dull	.47	.44
3. Church Atmosphere Attracts New Members	.43	.30
4. Visitors Feel Church is Warm and Friendly	.37	.45
5. Preaching Attracts New Members	.34	.41
6. Church is Warm and Friendly	.33	.45
7. Satisfied with Singing	.30	.34

Descriptions never do justice to an experience, but the most consistent term used to describe a growth climate is "celebrative." Other terms like "uplifting," "joyful," and "inspiring" are adjectives related to the celebration motif. Participants in well-developed celebrative assemblies can relate to the Psalmist's words, "Make a joyful noise to the Lord, all the lands! Serve the Lord with gladness! Come into his presence with singing" (Psa. 100:1-2).

C. Kirk Hadaway's study of Southern Baptist breakout churches found the same results. The strongest worship variable was "celebration."[2] Breakout churches had a significantly higher percentage (76%) indicating that celebration was always or usually evident in their worship services as compared to plateaued churches (47%). He also found other related descriptions that were statistically significant such as "expectation," "enthusiasm," and "joy."[3]

Not everyone likes the celebrative style of worship. Reverence and quiet reflection strongly suit some church members, and that is fine. Theological support is available for both sides of the continuum—reverence or celebration. Worship actually consists of different moods. Allen and Borror, in *Worship: Rediscovering the Missing Jewel,* identified joy, reverence, and faith as three different mood expressions.[4] Each is important in expressing worship to God.

While worship should have some ebb and flow, an important mood in New Testament worship fits the celebration motif. This is not to say that worship assemblies must predominantly fit one particular style. God is pleased with sincere worship in any style (from any culture) that does not violate clear biblical principles, but some teachers still theologize their preferred style and castigate all others as sinful. Therefore, a few observations from notable scholars are offered as a balance to demonstrate that "celebration" is just as acceptable to God as reverence and formality.

Allen and Borror draw this conclusion about worship:

> As a thoughtful gift is a celebration of a birthday, as a special evening out is a celebration of an anniversary, as a warm eulogy is a celebration of life, as a sexual embrace is a celebration of a marriage—so a worship service is a celebration of God.[5]

Everett Ferguson, Greek scholar and author of *Early Christians Speak,* has this to say about first century Christian worship:

Since the Lord's day was the day of the resurrection, Christian sources often identified it as a day of joy. . . . This was a pervasive note in contrast to the Sabbath. The rabbis stressed joy in connection with the Sabbath, but the Jewish customs for the Sabbath seemed somber to outside observers.[6]

Other scholars have drawn similar conclusions. New Testament professor Ralph P. Martin writes:

Essential Christian praise will be celebratory in tone. The style of worship under the new covenant is not mournful but joyous; it is a festive gathering to which we are invited (Heb. 12:22) as the firstborn of God's children gathered in holy array.[7]

As an intellectual concept, early Christian celebration does not threaten anyone, but the contemporary idea conjures up some disturbing images, especially for older church members. Concerns surface over uncontrolled emotions, a compromise of objective biblical truth, and a long list of abuses by some television evangelists. These fears are most often unfounded. Every church in this study was a non-charismatic, conservative, and traditional church. The biggest difference between growing and declining congregations was not what they did—they did about the same things—rather it was how they did it. Growing churches do a better job!

Dynamic assemblies are not a chance occurrence. They are the product of prayer, planning, variety, and the pursuit of excellence. A. W. Tozer considered worship the "missing jewel of the evangelical church." In some ways this is still true. Everyone affirms the preeminence of worship, but the actual time invested in preparing meaningful worship assemblies reveals that, for many churches, excellence in worship is the missing jewel. Preachers will invest ten or fifteen hours in sermon preparation while the remaining worship activities are pulled together just minutes before the assembly starts. Members and visitors are adversely affected; visitors do not return and members develop low morale.

Another consequence from the lack of quality preparation is the dilemma of predictability. After doing things the same way for so long, church members theologize their methods. Patterns are so deeply ingrained and comfortable, they must be the only biblical and acceptable patterns of worship. If anyone doubts this scenario, just change the order of worship and watch the response. Members may not articulate their responses in theological terms, but their reaction to small changes exposes a sacred attachment to established patterns of methodology.

Variety in worship is a major ingredient for a celebrative assembly, but without quality preparation variety is the first item lost and sameness becomes the theologically supported norm. So, if changes are unacceptable, all that is needed in worship preparation is to pick the songs and plug in the right people. At this point, churches have institutionalized poor quality and predictability.

Now the dilemma is based on the predictability principle: "The greater the predictability, the lower the impact." Churches have ensured sameness that produces boring, lifeless, and ritualistic services. Repetition of any kind causes people to mentally check out. It takes some variety to keep people interested and engaged. Consultant and author Herb Miller recognizes that "growing churches develop structured variety. Dying churches develop routine ruts."[8] He should know. Miller consults with one of the fastest declining denominations—Christian Church (Disciples of Christ). Some of their congregations, however, have discovered the way out of the dilemma. Worship must receive top priority through prayer, planning, variety, and the pursuit of excellence. They have rediscovered the missing jewel (well-prepared assemblies) and a vital factor for spiritual and numerical growth.

Warm and Friendly

Every normal person desires friendliness and warmth from fellow human beings. From birth to death, the journey is made rewarding by those special people who can warmly connect. No wonder Jesus said, "By this all men will know that you are my disciples, if you have love for one another"(John 13:35). Christian love runs deeper than warm and friendly, but these characteristics are a vital part. It should be no surprise that people are attracted to warm and extroverted congregations while they are repelled by indifferent members and internal church conflicts.

Danny McKinney conducted a religious survey among young adults in the Memphis area. He personally interviewed 107 individuals; about half were active in a church and the other half were uninvolved. A key question was asked, "If you were looking for a church in this area, what kind of things would you look for?" Both the active and inactive said they would look for a "loving fellowship." This was the dominant response without a close second.[9]

Church members participating in our study were asked to identify their congregational strengths. Without exception, both growing and declining churches listed their number one strength as friendly and loving. Another set of questions allowed members to evaluate the level of friendliness among themselves and toward visitors. Here a distinction surfaced between growing and declining churches. Growing churches are significantly more warm and friendly among themselves and toward visitors (compare Table 4.2).

Two types of friendliness determines church climate —inward friendliness and overflow friendliness. An inward type exists in all churches. Regardless of the conditions, people who stay with a congregation build a close network of relationships with a select few. While members see themselves as warm and caring, visitors evaluate the atmosphere as cool and aloof. Both evaluations are correct. Members become preoccupied with a few close friends, and visitors are left to find their way out.

Overflow friendliness is the second kind, and it is the type that predicts growth. Members need genuine and generous affirmation from staff, elders, and one another. Then outreach to visitors is possible as a natural overflow of Christian warmth and hospitality. This does not exclude the wise choice of using organized ministries such as greeters and visitation. They should compliment a congregation's spontaneous warmth.

Growing churches evaluated their climate as more than warm and friendly; they also saw it as accepting and non-judgmental. Churches develop a deeper level of attitudes that run beneath the surface of initial visitor treatment. The overall climate is either positive or negative, and *young adults are extremely sensitive,* with a strong bias for the positive.

Participants in the study evaluated their church's climate on a continuum from accepting of those who differ to narrow and critical. This climate variable produced the strongest correlation with growth and young adults (compare Table 4.2).

Churches of Christ are working against a well-developed but now unproductive focus. F. LaGard Smith's assessment of our condition is on target. He says, "Our focus on the church was a well-intended effort to counter denominationalism with its many departures from biblical pattern, but we concentrated on such things as the organization, work, worship, and name of the church, rather than on the power of the gospel, the cross of Christ, and our individual relationship with God."[10] I would add that an inordinate amount of time was spent on criticizing other traditions in the countering process, but criticism is like leaven. It leavens the whole lump and a critical spirit then pervades the whole church climate.

When negativism characterizes the church's climate, it has a chilling effect on members and ministry. Any new idea or new ministry becomes suspect as social gospel, gimmicks, or following a different tradition. It reminds me of the saying, "Everyone has gone to pot except you and me, and I am worried about you!" Members in this environment become discouraged because traditional ministry is not working and new suggestions get shot down. The only safe work is the ministry of criticism. Study findings indicate that such a climate is self-defeating. Members are leaving negative churches in large numbers and these congregations lack the ability to attract new members.

Growing churches are not avoiding the tough issues. They have learned how to address concerns by using a constructive approach. It does not matter if the issue is low member involvement or poor giving. The approach is charged with positive messages to motivate people. It is summed up this way, "The effect of a positive atmosphere is simple but decisive: What is happening here is *good*, not bad; *positive*, not negative; *helpful*, not another disappointment."[11] A non-critical, accepting, and positive climate is a choice that can determine a church's growth potential.

Growth Sounds

Student ministers usually aspire to great oratory that can captivate an audience. They feel they must become communicators capable of earth-shaking messages that qualify them for the lectureship circuit. This pressure intensifies the already challenging task of presenting biblical truth. How justified is such anxiety-producing pressure? Just how important is spectacular oratory for church growth?

Having dynamic speaking skills in the pulpit is a definite advantage for preachers and churches. The good news is that it is not that important for church growth. Actually, it is great news for preachers and churches because there are few Robert Schullers and Charles Swindolls among us to go around. Average communicators doing above average jobs of preparation and delivering relevant messages will get the job done.

Members in the Center's study registered their satisfaction level with the preaching in their congregation. Only a moderate correlation existed between membership satisfaction and church growth. Results changed, however, when members responded to the statement, "Our preaching attracts others to place membership with us." Preaching that can attract new members is a significant predictor of growth.

As with the worship assembly, membership satisfaction with the preaching is different from the ability to attract new members. It is a matter of the preferences of existing members in contrast to the preferences of potential new members. Most potential new members come from the post-war generation.

Post-war adults have offered very blunt but piercing evaluations of today's typical worship services and sermon messages. They consider the average message to be boring and irrelevant to everyday life. So many pollsters have tested the pulse of young adults that the guesswork is over. Their voices are clear and consistent enough to sound like a broken record. For example, Danny McKinney discovered this same response when he asked young people in the Memphis area, "Why do you think most people don't attend church?" The top response was it is "irrelevant."[12] Churches must try to understand the causes behind the negative evaluations.

McKinney also asked the question, "What could a minister do for you?" Guess what they said. "Make the Bible relevant." Post-war adults are hungry to hear biblical messages, but most of all they want to know how it can help them live better lives and cope with life's stresses. Preachers and teachers should consider spending half of their teaching time directly with the text and the remainder invested in relevant application.

Wise expositors would do well to know their post-war adult audience. Through no fault of their own, many are slightly media maimed and left-brain crippled. Television, movies, and video games have created a visually-oriented generation with very short attention spans. An average sentence in seventeenth century literature averaged over forty words; now the average sentence is less than twenty words.[13] It is unreasonable to expect post-war adults to follow long rational discourses, long assemblies, and lengthy sermons. Pre-war adults are also becoming less tolerant of long services and lengthy sermons.

Hopefully, the findings from this study will help preachers refocus on productive priorities rather than complicate an already difficult job. Ministers in Churches of Christ have undergone a role shift from traveling evangelist to located preacher during the first half of this century.[14] As conditions continue to change, ministers and members are struggling with an identity crisis for preachers. What are their roles and responsibilities? Research findings can offer some insights into the practical and growth-producing roles for ministers.

Preachers have always held a vital role in church growth. The Alban Institute conducted a study on new church members. In each church sample, the preacher was mentioned as an important attracting factor, and over 60% of the new members listed the preacher as the most important reason. His ability to attract new members was based on three qualities: first, good sermons; second, warmth; and third, spiritual depth.[15]

Kirk Hadaway's study is the most thorough analysis of the preacher's role and responsibilities that contribute to growth. His summary is concise and every sentence reveals what is not and what is a significant growth predictor:

The catalytic role of the pastor should be clear in all the research findings which have been reviewed in this chapter. Few pastors have the native ability to grow a church primarily through the force of their preaching or administrative acumen. And, in fact, sheer excellence in these areas is not required. Instead, pastors of growing churches are optimistic, evangelistic, and ambitious. They are pacesetters; they place a great emphasis on the Bible in their preaching; and they are able to generate enthusiasm. They direct their churches toward activities which will result in growth.[16]

These findings relate to the chapter on leadership. Preachers can survive without great oratory skills, but a church is not likely to grow unless the pulpit is used to give a growth focus to the body. Hadaway found that a preacher with vision and goal directedness correlated with growth.[17] In addition, he found that preachers of growing churches generated enthusiasm and kept the morale high. The most consistent and effective avenue to address these issues is through pulpit communication.

A helpful suggestion for leaders is to poll their young adults concerning worship. The recommendation is that they sit down together and discover what changes are needed so that post-war adults would invite their friends to the assembly. Growth depends on the ability of the church to attract new members, and the main source is friends of the existing young adult attendees. Growth potential dramatically increases if post-war members feel positive enough about the assembly to invite a guest.

Do not use this recommendation unless the leadership is committed to use the member input. Otherwise, leadership credibility is damaged and members become reticent to offer additional feedback. Leaders should glean the recommendations and develop a responsible plan to implement as many suggestions as possible. Of course, churches must decide which suggestions are acceptable. Here is a sample list of responses gathered by one congregation, and each item received high priority from the young adult participants:

1. Make the worship services more joyous and uplifting.
2. Allow more freedom to express joy, e.g., clapping.
3. Have more emotion and spontaneity in worship.
4. Welcome visitors with more friendliness.
5. Provide variety in the singing through special singing groups, solos, and contemporary songs.

Another significant growth predictor surfaced with this statement: "There is a contagiousness about our people, and a sense of expectancy which attracts and holds newcomers." Responses in the above example are a good description of a contagious atmosphere that attracts young adults. Music takes about 40% of worship time and is a key ingredient for setting a contagious growth climate.

At this juncture, numerous churches come to an impasse. James Emery White, in *Opening the Front Door,* warns that "people guard their taste in music more dearly than doctrine."[18] I have observed that members will defend doctrine and their music preferences with equal fervor. Understanding how taste develops is crucial. Pre-war adults, in their formative years, grew up hearing the old favorites over and over. After years, hearts and emotions become attached to traditional songs that can stir a lifetime of memory and these songs become as sacred as the Scripture they often quote.

Churches now face a predicament because of a major divergence in music styles. Post-war adults grew up with a style in popular and religious music that is *very* different from the traditional. White observes, "Listening to contemporary radio stations supports such a claim, for there you have 'eighth-notes,' while the church continues to play and sing in 'half-notes.'"[19] Contemporary religious music is faster, much more upbeat, and tends to "speak directly *to* God rather than singing *about* God."[20]

While attending a training seminar on contemporary worship, I had the chance to solicit members' reactions. An older couple there quietly listened and observed; so I asked them for an evaluation of contemporary music. They responded, "It didn't sound like worship music." This was an honest response with no attempt to devalue the music. But what does worship music sound like? For any particular person, it sounds like whatever style music he or she grew up with or has become accustomed to.

The impasse or predicament is how to incorporate both styles and keep everyone happy. If a church has a balanced membership in age, then balance in styles should receive consideration. First, poll the young adults as suggested earlier. Go slowly; give plenty of reasons before implementing any changes regardless of how small. *Never* surprise a congregation with worship innovations. Always expect some resistance. Based on an understanding of pre- and post-war adult preferences and needs, churches can implement gradual changes to develop a balance in worship styles.

Churches have clear choices when it comes to worship. They can choose to serve the dominant church culture without regard for reaching the post-war generations or they can work toward a balanced worship that can attract new members. Such assemblies are exciting, warm and friendly, relevant, and balanced in music styles.

Chapter Five

Involvement Choices

    All size churches, growing and declining, have a "revolving door" problem. Consider this condition by visualizing the revolving glass doors still found in some department stores. People flow in and flow out or trickle in and trickle out continuously. Every congregation has a similar revolving door for members. Each week they gain some and they lose some. Leaders are praying that the gains exceed the losses.

    Unlike the prominent revolving doors in a department store, church doors are less obvious. As new members enter the door, everyone is made aware by announcements and fanfare. The loss of members, however, is most often a quiet and imperceptible event. When engaged in church activities, those in attendance are usually very involved in socializing to the extent that absent members go undetected. The losses can continue unnoticed and unmeasured for years and possibly decades. Frequently, it takes a major crisis before the revolving door problem is analyzed and confronted.

    There is a better way. By keeping accurate records from week-to-week, leaders have the means of evaluating trends and addressing concerns before they develop into a crisis.

Each chapter suggests data categories for accurate record keeping and the findings presented offer a basis for comparisons. Accurate data on membership trends, for example, is essential for analyzing the revolving door problem.

Annual Membership Gains and Losses

Membership trends are significantly different for growing and declining churches. Figure 3 shows the average gains and losses for growing churches (Group A) compared to the results for declining churches (Group B). Group A had annual membership gains of 19% compared to only 10% for Group B. As expected, the percentage of annual gains correlated very strongly with overall growth (r = .71). Growing churches are able to attract nearly twice as many new members as declining churches.

While growing churches receive more new members through the front door, they also lose more members out the back door. Group A had annual membership losses of 16% compared to 11% for Group B. Figure 3 reveals the drastic differences between growing and declining churches in both gains and losses.

Did your congregation grow or decline in membership last year? Annual growth rates provide the bottom-line answer. These figures are the net results of combining gains and losses. For example, growing churches in our study averaged 3% annual membership growth and declining churches averaged 1% annual membership decline. By considering annual growth rates alone, churches miss critical growth issues.

FIGURE 3

Average Annual Membership
Gains and Losses (A)

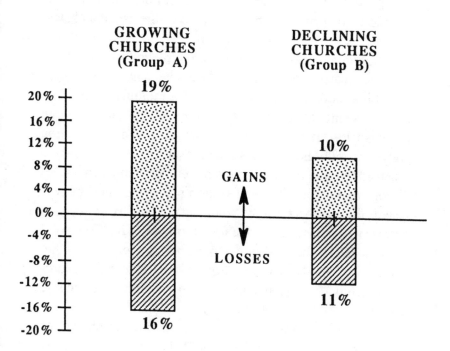

Gains and losses are two different components of growth. What affects one does not always affect the other. Churches should see them as two different areas requiring different ministry strategies. The requirements to attract a new member may not be sufficient to keep that person. Each chapter addresses significant variables that contribute to one or both components. These insights are useful for designing specific strategies to open the front door (increase the gains) and close the back door (decrease the losses).

In Figure 4, gains and losses are broken down into three important categories. Churches should keep accurate records in each area on a weekly or at least a monthly basis. New members enter the congregation in three ways, and a church can also lose members in three ways. The dotted section above the mid-line indicates the percentage of new members received through baptizing church members' children, called biological growth. The same section below the mid-line represents the members lost by biological death. Striped sections represent members who have transferred in or out. The solid section above the mid-line represents conversions of the unchurched and the solid section below the mid-line represents members who have left their church and have become inactive.

Membership transfers make up an important part of gains. Transfers account for 12% of the gains in Group A, which is nearly double the percentage for Group B (6.5%). This represents over half of the total gains for both groups: 63% for growing churches and 65% for declining churches.

Transfer growth is not a dirty word. Some in-town members do shift around from one congregation to another, but they are a small part of membership trends. Churches should not fear losing members to other congregations. Relevant and meaningful ministry will eliminate most of the shift. Church specialists have pointed out that "you can't steal well-fed sheep" and research suggests that satisfied members

FIGURE 4

Average Annual Membership Gains and Losses (B)

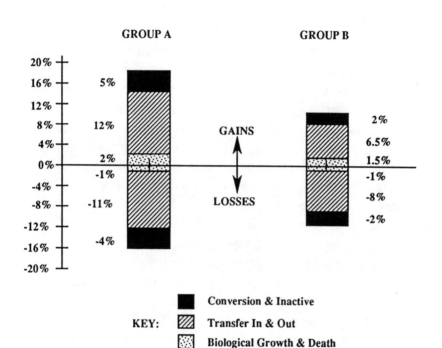

are not likely to shop around. New residents to the community, on the other hand, will look for a church with quality ministry. Because of high mobility, churches should expect and prepare for new members by transfer. An excellent preparation step is adequate staffing, which strongly correlated with gains (r = .41) and net growth (r = .51).

Another very strong predictor of gains came as a pleasant surprise—baptisms-to-membership ratio (r = .64). Evangelism results are presented in the next chapter. However, membership trends introduce the findings on baptisms. It is a surprise from the standpoint of conventional wisdom which tends to overlook evangelism as a growth factor.

Group A had 2% biological growth compared to 1.5% for Group B, but the significant difference is in the percentage of unchurched baptisms. Growing churches had more than twice as many conversions as declining churches. For Group B, only one in five new members (20%) was by conversion while Group A had one in four (26%). Effective evangelism is a predictor of gains and net growth.

Conversion growth from baptizing the unchurched will continue to increase in strength as a predictor of growth. Due to changing cultural conditions, transfer growth will be more difficult to achieve. Already, a shopping mentality pervades the Christian community. Add to this reality a post-war generation with weaker institutional ties, and churches are now faced with doing a better-than-average job to reach the potential transfers. Church growth depends on effective efforts for both transfer and conversion growth.

Conditions will become more challenging as the last group of receptive baby boomers age into the stability years. The youngest boomers turn 30 in 1994, and receptivity diminishes with age. Growth correlated best with the 20 to 29 age range ($r = .45$) and dropped with the 30 to 39 age range ($r = .27$). After these two age groups, there were no positive correlations with growth. The 20 to 29 age range represent the baby bust generation born between 1965 and 1976, and they number only half the size of the boomers. Churches will have a shrinking pool of transfers as boomers age and busters become the smaller and more secular target. With these imminent conditions, evangelism will become a necessity for church growth.

Churches do a fair job of tracking membership gains, but very little is done to track losses. Rarely will a church know the percentage of losses due to inactive members as opposed to members who transfer out. Consequently, the breakdown of losses in Figure 4 is based on a smaller sample of congregations with accurate data while the total gains and losses in Figure 3 and the breakdown of gains in Figure 4 are based on the total study sample.

Membership losses are the invisible dimension of growth. People are seldom aware of the degree of losses unless a crisis has surfaced the facts, and even informed churches lack a strategy to close the back door. Most congregations can anticipate a 1 to 2% annual loss through death. In the U.S. there are 1.2 deaths per 100 individuals. Mobility and church shopping will also make some losses unavoidable. A loss of 16%, however, is beyond a reasonable range for losses. Both growing and declining churches can reduce their losses if they take the responsibility to assimilate new and existing members seriously. Back door losses can be reduced in two ways: improve the group life and the involvement level of the membership. With front door and back door strategies, growing churches can increase the average 3% annual growth rate to a 5-9% range.

Opening wide the front door requires a broad range of ministries and church events where members can bring friends who are potential new members. Beyond the worship assembly, churches are using holiday activities, specialized seminars, and felt-need ministries to introduce their guests to Christians and Christian community. More activities mean more contacts and more potential new members.

Closing the back door requires only two ministry areas. Assimilating a new member requires either getting a person into a *group* where he or she can enjoy ongoing Christian community or by helping a new member locate a *job* of service in the congregation. So, closing the back door happens through groups and jobs.

Churches need a well-organized effort to accomplish both ministries. Most new members assimilate quickest through a meaningful group activity such as Bible classes and small home groups. On the other hand, a large percentage of pre-war adults who transfer tend to prefer a job assignment or a task-oriented ministry team. Churches can improve their annual growth rates by strategies both to improve group life and to increase membership involvement.

Groups

Each church in the sample was required to provide the necessary data for a thorough infrastructure analysis. A church's infrastructure consists of the various groups that meet on a regular basis such as Bible classes, ministry teams, recreational teams, and small home groups. In order to qualify, each group must have the capacity to facilitate some level of relationship bonding, which is a key ingredient for assimilation. Some gatherings are duplications of the same group and should be counted as one group. For example, a church may have a singles' Bible class on Sunday morning and Wednesday night; these groups are counted only once. An effective infrastructure will have more groups, offering more opportunities for members to build friendships and develop a sense of belonging. From the study results, groups-to-membership ratio surfaced as a strong predictor of growth (r = .44). Win Arn is a leading advocate for healthy group ratios. He recommends that churches have at least 7 adult groups for every 100 members. Each group is a "face-to-face fellowship of persons (normally ten to thirty) who meet at least monthly."[1]

Arn's recommendations are on target, and to my knowledge this study is the first to validate his ratios. Growing churches averaged 6 groups per 100 members while declining churches averaged only 4 groups per 100 members. Having an adequate number of adult groups is a predictor of growth. Also, the significance of a healthy infrastructure held up in a multivariate context. That is, four variables together offer the best explanation for growth: the worship assembly's ability to attract new members, adequate staffing, evangelism, and groups-to-membership ratio (see Table B.1 in Appendix B). *Churches should consider placing these items as top priorities.*

Analyzing infrastructure and having the correct number of groups are a beginning, but they are not enough. How groups function is equally important. Study findings suggest that ministry "effectiveness" is a critical component for growth.[2] For groups, this means having measurable goals for evaluating effectiveness. For example, the Southern Baptists have grown from twelfth place in size during the 1940s to the largest denomination in the U.S. by implementing a strategic Sunday school program. The classes that grow have specific goals to evangelize, educate, and assimilate. Most churches, to the contrary, tend to underutilize their groups by having only one purpose and no measurable goals.

In addition to group ratios, a moderate correlation was found in the percentage of the morning worship assembly that attended a Bible class (r = .29). Growing churches averaged 76% in a Bible class compared to 68% in declining churches. While most Churches of Christ have not used the Bible class as a growth strategy, it has served as a major avenue for jobs and building relationships.

Churches can improve the effectiveness of group life (regardless of the type of group) by using a few basic principles. These insights are simple, but leaders should know that implementation could face resistance. For years churches have operated with a self-directed ministry approach. Members receive an assignment such as teaching a Bible class. Then, no goals are set, there are no lines of accountability, and no follow-up procedures are in place. Volunteers become accustomed to receiving assignments and being left alone.

Principles for effectiveness require staff supervision, group member cooperation, goals, and progress evaluation. Such activities are foreign to numerous congregations and staff. Churches moving away from self-directed ministry could experience an awkward startup or even overt resistance from members. It could take some churches three to five years to work through the resistance and the period of awkward application before developing growth-producing ministry. Research support for organizational excellence is offered to encourage a long-term commitment for transitioning from a self-directed approach to effective ministry. The information is also a supplement to the extended discussion of infrastructure and group dynamics in *Church Growth Through Groups.*

Managing Groups

Self-directed ministry tends to follow the path of least resistance. In an educational setting, classes become preoccupied with listening to lectures and, in a service setting, ministries concentrate entirely on accomplishing a task. Each does a single good work, but groups fail to reach their full potential for ministry. Breaking away from a single-focused, nongrowth orientation requires group management and supervision in at least four areas.

1. **Purpose.** Groups can accomplish a wide range of ministry such as worship, teaching, fellowship, and evangelism. Without a clear purpose and intentional efforts, groups will focus on one activity to the exclusion of others. Growth-producing ministries identify their objectives, design appropriate strategies, and become intentional by setting specific and measurable goals.

Kirk Hadaway found a significant difference in breakout churches compared to plateaued congregations. For example, Sunday school in growing churches received a renewed emphasis, set growth goals, did prospect visitation, developed an accepting atmosphere for newcomers, and conducted worker training classes.[3] These kinds of characteristics differentiate well-managed ministry from self-directed efforts. Growth-oriented groups discard an inward self-serving focus by adopting multiple ministry objectives that include reaching out to potential new members. Each group leader receives training in effective growth strategies and groups are led in the goal-setting process.

Purpose-driven ministry represents a major but positive change for congregations. Leaders are first faced with the decision of where to begin. Most traditional growing churches are using one or more of three options for intentional group ministry: Sunday school, ministry teams, and small home groups. Where to begin is best determined by the needs and attitudes of members, staff, and the community. Numerous books and workshops are available for understanding the organizational details of the different options.[4] Congregations would benefit most by perfecting one option before trying a second.

2. *Size*. Both small and middle-size groups have a workable attendance range that allows members to build relationships and include new people. Middle-size gatherings of people allow for surface or secondary interaction and work well with fifteen to forty participants. Small gatherings allow members to go beyond surface relationships, and function best with six to twelve participants. Without management, groups increase in size beyond the comfortable range for relationship building and assimilating new members. They become closed due to numerical saturation and exhibit an exclusionary atmosphere undetected by most members.

It is possible that the most powerful motivator for leaders to take group management seriously is recognizing the biblical emphasis on Christian community and *fellowship*. From the very beginning Scripture declares, "And they devoted themselves to the apostles' teaching and *fellowship*, to the breaking of bread and the prayers" (Acts 2:42). The first Christians were devoted to fellowship, which refers to sharing both their material goods and their very lives.

God added thousands of new converts to a new family, which implied meaningful new relationships. Missiologist Allen Tippett believes that "evangelism which pulls individuals out of their familiar contexts and provides no new context is 'half-baked' and may well do more harm than good."[5] An effective new context is a nonsaturated group where new members (converts and transfers) can make new friends. People need the church's help through structured and managed opportunities to experience the divine blessing of fellowship.

On a spiritual plane, God created fellowship through the redemptive work in Christ Jesus (I John 1:1-3). However, on a physical plane, fellowship is experienced through human interaction in the form of relationships. Misunderstanding this is to miss a key principle of membership assimilation. Michael Donahue and Peter Benson, in a study of 492 congregations, found the most powerful predictor of growth was when churches helped members make friends.[6] Friendship ties are a glue that bonds members to the congregation and facilitates the experience of divine fellowship. Managing the size of groups can improve the opportunities for building Christian community and closing the back door.

3. *Age.* Groups reach saturation due to size, and they also become closed with aging. After about twelve months, most groups lose their ability to add new members. Research cited by consultant Carl George suggests that 50% of groups designed to increase and become two groups can do so within a year. After two years the rate dramatically drops to 5%.[7]

What happens to the internal dynamic as the group ages? What causes an exclusionary atmosphere to develop? A new group starts without established relationships. Members are open and ready to build friendships. Making friends takes time and effort, and after months new relationships are forged. With the passing of time, the ties between members become tighter and tighter to the point that it is very difficult for a new member to push his or her way into a tight network of relationships. New members are not inclined to force their way into groups in the first place; instead they anticipate some help or they leave. An invisible barrier of exclusiveness has developed making the group saturated regardless of size.

4. *Facilities.* Finally, crowded room conditions affect growth. Having a full room is a psychological boost, but it hinders the addition of any new people and it discourages member attendance. Crowded space may seem too obvious to consider, but a casual observation of Bible classes and small home groups will demonstrate that this principle is routinely ignored. Leaders could improve group life by monitoring group size and space and managing the groups to create conditions for growth.

These four management principles, along with group ratios, provide leaders the tools to analyze their congregation's infrastructure. Like individual groups, the entire infrastructure can become too closed for effective assimilation. If a church lacks enough groups or if the existing groups are unintentional, too large, too old, and crowded for space, something can be done to correct these conditions. Proper actions start with an accurate assessment of the existing groups (infrastructure), and the process requires at least an annual review.

Multiplying Groups

If an infrastructure is saturated and closed, the best response is to start new groups. All groups will naturally move toward the saturation point due to size or age. The productive solution is a strategy to start new groups on a quarterly or annual basis. Church size and the number of new member additions will determine the frequency. As a rule, for every ten to fifteen new members, a congregation could use a new group.

Church growth specialists call this the "new unit principle." As explained earlier, new groups grow faster because all members are on equal footing for building relationships. The new unit principle applies to all aspects of ministry. New churches, new ministries, new classes, and new small groups tend to grow faster. Kirk Hadaway discovered that breakout churches (plateaued for five years, then grew) were more likely to have started new groups the previous twelve months than the plateaued congregations.[8] Therefore, having the correct number of groups and starting new ones correlate strongly with growth.

Win Arn recommends one out of five adult groups in the church should be new.[9] Start by developing groups for young adults and new members. Long-tenured members may offer the greatest resistance to change. It is more productive to work with groups that are open to innovation and represent the most receptive population segment for new members.

The pyramid principle is a time-honored illustration demonstrating the need for expanding leadership. If a pyramid is to increase in size, the first step is to increase the size of the base. Likewise, to grow a church (pyramid height), the first action is to increase the number of leaders (the pyramid base). However, this is an inadequate concept for Christian community. It leaves out the reality that leaders function in and through groups, and group settings are the context for locating and developing new leaders. A better concept emerges by seeing the pyramid base as leaders working in groups. For church growth, design strategic efforts to increase the number of groups and leaders.

Jobs

Each church in the sample provided information indicating the number of members with and without job assignments. Data was limited to designated task responsibilities for congregational ministry. Growing churches had a slightly higher average with 41% of their members assigned to one or more jobs compared to 39% for declining churches. The difference between the groups produced a very weak correlation with growth.

Growing congregations are primarily reaching the 20 to 39 age range, and their time-stressed lifestyles are making the job of assimilation more challenging. Meaningful groups are providing the quickest avenue to start the assimilation process. All new members, however, should receive encouragement to exercise their stewardship responsibility of serving the body (Eph. 4:11-12; I Pet. 4:10). Effective assimilation is best accomplished by involving new members in a group and by assigning a job.

Job assignments did prove important in closing the back door. Job-related involvement levels demonstrated a moderate relationship in reducing annual membership losses (r = .29). Getting more members involved in serving the body can help reduce the membership losses and improve the overall growth rate.

Involvement is a broader concept than just having a job. Flavil Yeakley's ground-breaking work found involvement to be a significant predictor of growth when it included:

1) the average percentage of members in attendance at the regularly scheduled services of the congregation;
2) the percentage of members having a leadership role in the congregation;
3) the percentage of members having a specific work assignment; and,
4) contributions per member per week—with one point counted for each ten cents in contributions.[10]

Flavil also discovered the importance of both how many jobs a church has available and how many jobs the members perceive as available. Growth related not only to the roles-to-member ratio, but also to the perceived roles-to-member ratio. Having enough jobs to go around is very important, but even more so is the need to clearly communicate their availability.[11]

Consultant Carl George recommends an involvement level target of at least 50%.[12] Any percentage below 40% results in a nongrowth condition. A church's size plays an important role in reaching involvement-level goals. Congregations under 200 members have an easier task of mobilizing members. As membership increases, the task becomes more difficult. In large churches 50% or more is possible, but involvement levels strongly depend on adequate staffing.

Professional staff have a critical role in organizing, recruiting, and motivating volunteers.

Having members actively working is a start, but the type of work makes a difference. Is it busy work or does it contribute to growth? Carl George recommends at least 10% of the members be involved in outreach-oriented activities. Any area of ministry qualifies if it is helping the unchurched become acquainted with Christians and Christian community. Involvement through groups and jobs enriches the lives of Christians, closes the back door, and makes a significant contribution to opening the front door.

Chapter Six

Outreach Choices

Most Christians who experience conversion to Christianity as an adult hold wonderful memories of the event. For them, the people who shared the Good News and the moment of decision become very special. Each case of an adult conversion recorded in the Book of Acts was surrounded by just such events. When the Ethiopian eunuch heard the Gospel from Philip and the Philippian jailer heard it from Paul, they were converted and the result was rejoicing —personal and emotional exuberance expressed by new Christians. From my own and other adult conversions, I know that it still happens today. The following story was shared by a friend who holds just such happy memories of his own conversion:

"Eleven years ago I met George, a former missionary to Greece. When I met him, he and his family had relocated back in the U.S. after having served sixteen years and he was now selling insurance (he sold me a policy). Though he was several years my senior, our families became friends and we enjoyed spending time together.

"I was amazed at how often George was able to work God into our conversation, but I never saw him as overbearing. He didn't push us to attend his church. He just continued to ask questions that made us think. Soon important events began to unfold. George invited my wife and me to share dinner with his family. Afterwards, he suggested that we play a little racquetball and—by the way—there was a Bible study at a friend's home that he wanted us to attend. Out of respect for our friendship, I told him, 'Okay, George, we'll come this *one* time.'

"The study was attended by a total of nine people. The discussion that took place as we studied made the Bible come alive as I had never known possible. On the way home, my wife and I found ourselves going over points of interest in the study and curious about next week's subject. We were hooked!

"After six weeks (we attended the Bible study regularly), George invited us to his office for lunch. He told me that he had something more important to talk about than insurance. He shared what the Bible said about sin, forgiveness, and God's plan for salvation. The next day my wife and I—with joy—responded to the Good News and became Christians."

What turned out as a wonderful conversion story involving special people and memorable events actually began as a situation fraught with risk. Where does a Christian like George—just as Philip and Paul demonstrated—find the courage to confront another human being with the divine claims of Christ? What would motivate someone to move beyond his or her comfortable Christian community and risk possible conflict, personal rejection, and perhaps the loss of a friend? (At certain times and places it could include risking one's life.)

The church growth movement has contributed more toward evangelism renewal than any other recent effort in North America. Reactions have ranged from high praise all the way to extreme criticism. Some writers have suggested that evangelism and growth are motivated by numerolatry (worship of numbers) and success mongering. In other words, people seek notoriety by increasing the numbers and flaunting it as success.

Nothing could be further from the truth. Christians like George find their deep-felt motivation from strong theological convictions. Scriptures—from Genesis to Revelation—reveal the heart and mind of God, and his will and commands for evangelism are numerous and explicit. Years and mountains of written academic debate have not shaken Churches of Christ from an evangelical commitment to make disciples of all nations (Matt. 28:18-20).

Also, churches have not forgotten that numbers represent souls facing an eternal destiny with or without Christ. As a twenty-one-year-old Christian convert, I once was a number. I do not remember if two or twenty baptisms were registered in the congregation that year. All I do know is that I thank God I was one of the numbers. Baptismal or attendance numbers are not crass nor are they symbols of success. They do represent precious souls and reflect a church's concern for God's mind and heart.

This chapter is not intended as a theological treatise. An abundance of books and articles address the topical and textual issues relevant to the church's mission.[1] Nor are the research findings offered as a pragmatic substitute for theology. Growth-minded congregations are frequently accused of doing things simply because they work (pragmatism) regardless of biblical truths (theology).

Feeding the poor, serving a neighbor, or teaching someone about Christ are examples of actions motivated by Scriptures whether they produce any measurable results or not. Christians should first ground all ministry activities through the theological enterprise. Hopefully, the research findings will encourage churches to do exactly that and I am confident that leaders will rediscover their God-given evangelistic mandate. The time is right—we have a receptive population of adults and there are effective methods available to reach them.

Study Findings

Whether it is evangelism, benevolence, or missions, each church action is a faith response to God's revelation. By God's design, however, evangelism produces measurable growth for the local church. Just as America's future depends on healthy families giving birth to a new generation, Christianity's future depends on churches having new births in Christ. Theology and basic logic should motivate churches to evangelistic action. And now, a growing body of research verifies the impact of evangelism on church growth.

As introduced in Chapter 5, baptisms-to-membership ratio produced a strong relationship with membership gains ($r = .64$) and overall growth ($r = .52$). All baptisms are included in this variable, both biological growth (baptisms of members' children) and conversion growth (baptisms of the unchurched). Group A averaged annually 7.1 baptisms per 100 members while Group B averaged 3.7 baptisms per 100 members (see Figure 5).

Our findings discovered over forty different factors related to numerical increase. Staff and members are taxed by an endless list of possible good works. So, how important is evangelism compared to so many other options? To answer this question, local institutional factors were subjected to multiple regression analysis. This helped identify which variables in a multivariate context were the strongest predictors of growth. As stated earlier, four institutional variables (what a church does) surfaced as significant predictors and baptisms-to-membership ratio was third in predictive efficacy. *This means that few activities in church ministry are more vital to church growth than evangelism.*

FIGURE 5

Average Annual Baptisms Per 100 Members

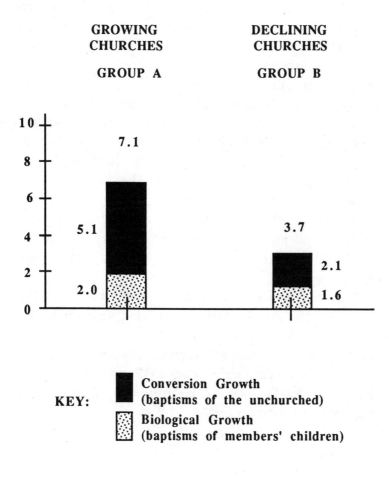

GROWING
CHURCHES

GROUP A

DECLINING
CHURCHES

GROUP B

KEY:

■ Conversion Growth
(baptisms of the unchurched)

▨ Biological Growth
(baptisms of members' children)

Some clarification is necessary at this point. Growing churches have a higher percentage of young married couples with children than declining churches. Is it possible that the higher baptisms-to-membership ratio in growing churches is *not* related to evangelism but could result from the larger number of young couples who transfer in and the normal biological growth from baptizing their pre-teen and early-teen children? If so, conventional wisdom would stand—growth primarily comes from transfers and children's baptisms.

Such a potential scenario prompted a closer analysis of baptisms-to-membership ratio for clarifying the issue. This variable includes all baptisms; therefore, baptisms were separated into two categories. Biological growth represents baptisms of members' children, and conversion growth quantifies the baptisms of individuals who are not children of church members, called the unchurched. They are two distinct categories because the types of ministry necessary to reach each are quite different. Members' children are frequently reached through the Bible class program and youth ministry, but reaching the unchurched requires very intentional evangelistic activities.

The additional analysis revealed that baptisms of the unchurched also produced a strong relationship with church growth ($r = .43$). In addition, unchurched baptisms had an almost perfect correlation with baptisms-to-membership ratio ($r = .94$), which means they measured the same thing when correlated to growth—the relationship of evangelism (conversion growth) to church growth.

Figure 5 gives a visual comparison for this critically important finding. There is little difference between Group A and B in the number of baptisms for members' children. (Group A averaged 2 per 100 members and Group B averaged 1.6 per 100 members). However, a significant difference exists between the two groups for baptisms of the unchurched. Growing churches had more than twice the conversions (5.1 per 100 members) than declining churches (2.1 per 100 members).

In response to the potential scenario given above, the higher baptisms-to-membership ratio for growing churches is not due to biological growth. Rather, growing churches are more successful in evangelism, resulting in conversion growth. *Again, this means that few activities in church ministry are more vital to church growth than evangelism.*

Until recently, social science research had not uncovered the powerful relationship between evangelism and church growth. Fortunately, this study does not stand alone. The latest collection of research projects reported in *Church and Denominational Growth* (Roozen and Hadaway) draws very similar conclusions. Perhaps, C. Kirk Hadaway has done more than anyone in recent years to focus attention on the significant role of evangelism. Based on his own and other research findings, he draws this remarkable conclusion: "Outreach seems to be the single most important action a church can take if it wants to grow. . . . In fact, this is the most consistent finding in this section."[2]

Evangelism Anxiety

Churches of Christ have a deep-seated conviction that evangelism should receive top ministry emphasis. Members were asked in the written survey to prioritize a list of fourteen ministry areas—first, by what they personally felt should be the most important and, second, by what emphasis they felt their local congregation placed on them. The collected responses produced a numerical value for each ministry. By comparing the differences in the two lists, the number one preference for an increased ministry emphasis for both growing and declining churches was evangelism.

A difference surfaced, however, between churches in Group A and Group B in their prioritized preference list.

Members of growing congregations felt that evangelism was the most important ministry while members of declining churches ranked evangelism third behind fellowship and preaching. *The degree of concern does appear to have an impact on the results.*

Churches of Christ have a strong conviction about evangelism, but for most congregations it is not happening on any intentional or consistent basis. Since the desire is present, we must then consider the possible reasons for such limited success.

George G. Hunter, III, consultant and professor from Asbury Theological Seminary, interviewed church members who were committed enough to attend his evangelism seminars but did not engage in evangelism. He discovered that most of them had more "hang-ups than the city art gallery!"[3] Their main problem was a stereotyped view of an evangelist (a personal worker who conducts evangelistic Bible studies). He identified four issues:[4]

1. Members visualized a personal worker as primarily confrontational and manipulative.
2. They felt that the evangelistic Bible study was designed to generate guilt and feelings of condemnation in the potential convert.
3. They believed that personal workers use rehearsed authoritarian presentations.
4. Last, members imagine the evangelist using a task-oriented monologue without a genuine interest in the potential convert's concerns.

No wonder these members would experience evangelistic schizophrenia. If someone else did the work, I would be all for it too. Happily, these are stereotypes and not reality. While these views may have characterized some past evangelism methods, present-day times and people have changed. Impersonal approaches of every kind produce meager results and discourage the majority of church members from participating in the ministry of outreach.

Effective evangelism is a slow and relational process. By "effective" I mean evangelism that results in higher baptismal and retention rates. It is relational in that new convert retention requires meaningful friendship ties between the convert and church members. Also, it is a slow process because it usually requires support from the church through a broad range of events where potential converts are introduced to Christ and Christian community over time. With this context in mind, George Hunter, III, offers a correct view of personal work:

1. Effective faith-sharing is more relational than verbal.
2. The evangelist does more listening than talking.
3. The evangelist vocalizes suggestions more than propositions.
4. Christianity is more caught than taught.
5. Conversion is almost never instant, but takes some weeks or months from insemination to new birth.
6. The occasions for evangelistic conversation usually arise situationally. The message is seldom a rehearsed theological formula out of a book or a packaged evangelistic program. It is usually specific, tailored to the recipient's felt need, point of openness, searching, or pain, and presents the facet of the gospel that is most immediately relevant.
7. In evangelism, the credibility, sensitivity, and skills of the communicator's human relations matter a great deal.[5]

Team Effort

Select a Method

C. Peter Wagner's medical model of effective ministry has seven vital signs of a healthy growing church. His sixth vital sign is *using an evangelistic method that works.*[6] Employing a specific method that produces results is paramount. Talking about evangelism, training for evangelism, having a few workers involved in evangelism is fine, but it is not enough. Kirk Hadaway, in his study of breakout churches, found the distinguishing difference in growing versus plateaued congregations was a major step beyond evangelistic desire and renewal; it was the ability to produce results.[7]

Churches should start by considering at least one or more proven methods that fit the congregation and community. The three most frequently used approaches are visitation evangelism, Sunday school evangelism, and small group evangelism. A full description of methods is available through a variety of resources such as books, videos, and workshops.[8]

Each method, when used efficaciously, has its own specific organization that utilizes the entire congregation as a support team and works as a process. Productive strategies stand in stark contrast to the antiquated "Lone Ranger" model. Evangelism relegated to a few workers and isolated from most church activities is doomed to low conversion numbers and high dropout rates. Hopefully, the reasons will be apparent from the following section on evangelism as a process.

Build a Supportive Atmosphere

In Chapter 4, a growth climate best experienced during the Sunday morning activities introduced the characteristics of a supportive atmosphere for growth. Such conditions are necessary to motivate membership participation that will ultimately lead to conversion growth. Table 6.1 presents the growth climate variables and their relationship to growth and baptisms, and each variable suggests specific areas requiring planned effort.

Churches develop a personality or climate over the years from one emphasis or another, and at times from no emphasis at all. A nongrowth personality is classified as an inward orientation emphasizing the needs of existing members. Frequently, inward orientations develop when leaders allow churches to slide into institutionalism where a clear sense of mission is lost. Whether it is sermon messages, Bible class lessons, or a church ministry, a continuous focus on either member needs or institutional needs persists. Members are seldom encouraged to extend their concerns beyond the immediate family—home and congregation. Church becomes a safe place to escape from the world, receive comfort, and fellowship with long-time friends.

On the other hand, a growth personality is an outward orientation emphasizing the needs of nonmembers as well as members. For members to risk bringing a friend to church-related activities, basic conditions of warmth, friendliness, and acceptance are essential. Asking an unchurched friend to a religious event is anxiety producing enough. Growth-oriented churches recognize the anxiety for members and visitors, and tirelessly work for a friendly and inclusive atmosphere for guests. Chapter 4 describes the elements of a growth climate surrounding an inclusive worship assembly and delineates the atmosphere necessary to reach a receptive population of young adults.

TABLE 6.1
Measurements of Growth Climate
Related to Baptisms

Variables	Correlation with Growth	Correlation with Baptisms-to-Membership Ratio
1. Church Accepts Others vs. Narrow and Critical	.50	.59
2. Church is Exciting vs. Dull	.47	.49
3. Church Atmosphere Attracts New Members	.43	.39
4. Visitors Feel Church is Warm and Friendly	.37	.39
5. Preaching Attracts New Members	.34	.30
6. Church is Warm and Friendly	.33	.36

Pulpit ministers hold the key position of influence and offer the greatest hope for assisting an inward-focused church to make a transition to an outward orientation and growth personality. Preachers, over a period of time, can help memers rediscover their evangelistic mandate through sermon messages, Bible class lessons, training sessions, and especially by modeling an evangelistic lifestyle.

If staff members have little heart for evangelism, the congregation is not likely to catch an evangelistic vision. Kirk

Hadaway's research firmly linked the role of staff in helping a church move from an extended plateau or decline to outreach and growth. Growing churches had staff that actively modeled outreach and reemphasized evangelism in their communications.[9]

Congregations can evangelize and grow if leaders (staff and elders) will take a proactive lead. They should select a method, build a supportive atmosphere, model an evangelistic lifestyle, and involve the entire church in the evangelism process. (Chapter 3 offers correlative recommendations for leaders.)

A Process

Flavil R. Yeakley's research, presented in *Why Churches Grow,* laid out the foundation for understanding the components of effective evangelism. It is more than an event; rather it is "the process of influencing others in such a way that the Christ who lives in Christians and in their message is formed in the lives of other people."[10] His findings serve as the starting point for understanding the process and implementing an effective evangelism method.

Process is defined as "a natural phenomenon marked by gradual changes that lead toward a particular result."[11] Concepts such as "natural" and "gradual" counter the stereotypical images of evangelism. Pictures of confrontation, manipulation, and rehearsed presentations are tossed out the window. They are replaced with natural qualities like friendship, patience, listening, and relevant sharing. Results from a process come a little slower than confrontational approaches, but the retention rate is dramatically higher.

Churches *can* organize their evangelistic efforts to facilitate the natural and gradual process. It involves three distinct strategies: entry points, pathways, and an invitation. Evangelism is frequently viewed in terms of verbal communication designed to persuade. Because numerous activities support evangelistic communication, the whole process can be classified as "outreach." What follows is a brief introduction of each strategy in the outreach process:

1. *Entry points* are activities where the unchurched can receive an introduction to many Christians, Christian community, and the Christian message. Churches need a wide variety of entry points in order to make contact with the largest number of potential new converts. Fewer entry points result in fewer contacts and vice versa.

Worship assemblies, Bible classes, small groups, recreational teams, specialized ministries for youth and singles, and felt-need seminars are just a few examples of possible entry points. Having them is a start, but the real threshold is broken when members actively invite unchurched people from their social networks to attend these well-designed entry points.

First, members must break out of the "us four and no more" mentality where activities are never imagined or designed for inclusion. Most church activities can serve as entry points if members are made aware of the process and how they can participate. Possibly the most important thing members can do to serve on the evangelistic team is invite unchurched friends to church activities and the second is to demonstrate friendliness toward all those invited by all other members.

2. *Pathways* are activities that meet on a weekly or at least monthly basis. Helping members and potential converts experience community and receive continued exposure to the Christian message are two of their major goals. Pathways can serve as entry points, but for an entry point to qualify as a pathway it must have an ongoing meeting schedule with opportunities for relationship building. For example, worship assemblies would not qualify as a pathway, but Bible classes, small groups, and special ministries could measure up if the

groups are managed properly. Effective pathways have several clear and well communicated goals. Chapter 5 describes the important group management issues.

A primary goal for pathways is to facilitate the making of friendship ties between group participants. Yeakley's study findings surfaced a key aspect on convert retention. He concludes that "when subjects formed personal relationships with members of the congregation, they were likely to remain faithful. When they did not form such personal relationships, they were likely to drop out of the church."[12] Christianity is deeply relational in nature and the analogy of the church as a family includes the vital functions of community and friendship.

Pathways also provide ongoing opportunities for the unchurched to receive exposure to the Christian message. Yeakley found that evangelistic results were significantly related to the number of exposures subjects had to the Christian message. Churches with the highest growth rates used more avenues of influence.[13] Effective evangelism is a process marked by gradual changes in both personal and group identification which require numerous exposures to Christian community and the Christian message.

3. *Invitations* are timely communication activities where a Christian persuades a potential convert publicly to accept the Lordship of Jesus Christ. As a process, invitations work best with the unchurched who participate in a pathway. Their bonding to Christian friends begins before the invitation and enhances their receptivity to the message and messenger. Timeliness is determined by the degree of relational bonding to group members.

Successful persuasion also depends on the potential convert's perceiving the personal worker as a friend.[14] Pathway activities allow the personal worker to develop friendship ties with regular attending visitors before an invitation is extended. Evangelistic communication usually takes place outside the group context, but success still depends on a genuine friendship style of nonmanipulative dialogue.[15]

Invitation activities are not always necessary in the evangelistic process. On occasion, individuals will make a decision privately and communicate a personal readiness to accept the Lordship of Christ publicly. However, experience indicates that most potential converts will wait for a personal invitation.

Churches have a choice of either facing the future hoping to remain vital from transfer and biological growth or building an outreach-focused church that is friendly, exciting, outward-oriented, and growing. Building an evangelistic church begins with proactive leadership. Leaders should select a method, build a supportive atmosphere, model an evangelistic lifestyle, and involve the entire church in the outreach process. They should identify members with the gift of evangelism, provide the needed training, and help them make contacts through pathways and entry point activities.

Chapter Seven

Identity Choices

Churches are like people in that they develop a personality or identity. For example, some congregations are energetic, warm, and friendly while others are inert, cool, and aloof. Understanding church personality, how it is formed, and how it can change is foundational for applying growth principles from previous chapters. This subject is last because it is the most crucial in affecting ministry selection and implementation. Congregational identity ultimately decides a church's future.

For a quick and lucid picture of church personality, talk with a few ministers who have worked with small rural congregations. They can tell stories of personally navigating through the members' unspoken behavioral expectations and family feuds that make a wartime minefield look safe. Distinctive identities are not limited, however, to small or rural churches. Every congregation has an identifiable personality.

Church location, age, and size, along with other integral factors such as historical roots and traditions, contribute to a church's personality. Nevertheless, not every dimension of identity equally affects a church's growth potential. Chapter 6 introduced the critical elements separating a growth from a nongrowth personality. A nongrowth personality is an inward orientation emphasizing the needs of existing members and the resulting exclusive atmosphere hinders growth. A growth personality is an outward orientation emphasizing the needs of nonmembers as well as members and the resulting inclusive atmosphere facilitates growth. Consequently, each orientation influences a church's response to ministry options and community conditions and that response ultimately determines growth potential.

Subcultures and Ministry Options

Because identity resides in the whole membership, it is also referred to as a *subculture*. Members will share similar cultural characteristics found in their local communities, but they also hold attitudes, values, and practices peculiar to their subculture. Each religious tradition and denomination tends to produce churches with similar subcultures even though some diversity exists within the tradition. Churches of Christ have a distinct subculture that nonmembers would notice if they visited a congregation anywhere in the U.S., and at the same time there are significant areas of diversity.

Researchers have identified some subcultures that are biased against ministry options such as church growth and evangelism while others are friendly toward these methodologies. Mainline liberal Protestant denominations exhibit the clearest and most blatant nongrowth subculture, which is a major factor in their numerical decline since the 1960s. The vast majority of growing churches have a conservative subculture; however, conservatism alone is not the bottom-line factor. Churches of Christ, for the most part, have conservative subcultures, but many are not growing. Again, an outward orientation is the key element for growth in a liberal or conservative subculture. Identifying different subcultures is an important start. To have some control in subcultural formation, it is necessary to understand the contributing factors to its development.

Researchers have also identified significant differences between conservative and liberal Protestant subcultures that explain their responses to ministry options and community conditions. Conservative churches are less affected by cultural trends; they maintain a distinction and separation from mainstream American culture as a witness to particular biblical convictions. Mainline liberal churches, on the other hand, "are embedded in a secular, pluralistic society. The values of religious tolerance and civility are deeply ingrained."[1] In other words, cultural trends like privatized religion and political correctness are high priorities in a mainline liberal subculture. Dean M. Kelly states it this way: "The cultural climate may indeed be a dominating causal factor in the growth or decline of mainline churches, which are apparently very susceptible to transient shifts in public opinion about what's 'in' and what's 'out' this decade, year, or month."[2] Researchers are concluding that each of these choices is a major contributor to growth or decline—decline for liberal subcultures and growth for some conservative subcultures.

Nowhere is the difference between the subcultures clearer than with evangelism. Conservative groups have held to the traditional view of "soul winning" and evangelism in spite of the fact that only a few have discovered a workable method. There remains a strong conviction that people face eternal separation from God without faith in Christ Jesus. To the contrary, mainline liberals have successfully de-emphasized evangelism because it is offensive to privatized religion and political correctness. Roy Oswald and Speed Leas, researchers with The Alban Institute, acknowledge that traditional evangelistic methods do not "respect an important norm of the religious culture of moderate and liberal congregations, which is that religion—and especially your own religious experience—is not something you speak aloud or boldly."[3] Their aversion to sharing Christ or their personal spiritual journey is so strong it is recognized as "a conspiracy of silence which is a part of the organizational norms of the mainline church."[4]

How can such a subculture develop? Bruce A. Greer traced the evangelism trends in the American Baptist churches from 1936 to 1991.[5] The denomination's direction was set by key individuals of influence who served a term as director of evangelism. The second office holder, Jitsus Morikawa (1956-76), epitomizes the means and especially the end results of a liberal agenda. Through mainline liberal hermeneutics, he simply changed the definition of evangelism. Greer summarized his change: "Evangelism is (1) God's mission and not the church's, (2) social, not simply individual, (3) sending the church into the world and not winning the world into the church."[6] With these changes, Morikawa removed all responsibility to confront anyone with the claims of Christ and evangelism became the church's presence in the world without regard for outcomes.

Could this or similar developments ever happen among Churches of Christ? Certainly, a conservative subculture characterizes most congregations; so why are so few churches evangelistic? Could other subculture aspects other than the conservative-liberal spectrum contribute to the situation? Herb Miller, author and executive director for the Christian Church (Disciples of Christ), delineates sixteen reasons why the mainline churches lost their evangelistic focus and concern for the Great Commission. Several of his reasons represent sober warnings to all conservative subcultures:

4. **Erosion of a Biblical Authority Base.** . . . When a personal-opinion authority base replaces a biblical authority base, we can discard with ease several clear priorities, such as "Go into all the world and make disciples." . . .

6. **Overreaction to Evangelism Excesses.** With justified rejection of revivalistic, "Elmer Gantry-type" manipulation from earlier in the century, many clergy threw the computer out the door along with the faulty software package.

7. **The "Rogerian Counseling Orientation."** This style of clergy leadership originated as an essential part of counseling training in the new and valuable pastoral-care movement that began in the early 1960s. . . . While this technique had immense value in therapeutic counseling conversations, many pastors adopted the Rogerian approach as a total leadership style. When applied to the evangelism mandate, this meant that they needed to wait in their churches and offices for people to come to them for help—rather than reaching outside the circle of church and office with any form of "Good News" proclamation.

11. **Preoccupation with *Didache*.** This view implies that teaching is the valid means of communicating Christ. When this thinking swept in—as a logical part of the American fascination with higher education—it subtly but effectively displaced the value previously placed on preaching, worship, and proclamation.

12. **Declining Emphasis of Evangelism in Seminaries.** Captivated by other important aspects of the faith—such as Christian education, social action, and counseling—a vacuum arose. Zero courses in evangelism became the norm. In some cases professors even spoke against evangelism or met questions regarding its importance with an academically raised eyebrow—viewing this discipline as an outdated habit from an antiquated past. . . .

16. **Antique Worship Services.** When church leaders have little or no "extroversion orientation," their motivation evaporates for developing worship services that attract and inspire young adults in the twenty-five to forty-five age range. Erroneously assuming that the same kind of

worship that "1950s model" young adults found meaningful still interests that age range today, tradition began to strangle effectiveness in many mainline worship services. The result: Young adults who found the services boring and irrelevant went elsewhere, or nowhere[7]

Churches of Christ can learn from the near fatal mistakes made by mainline liberal Protestants. Surely, no church wants to go through the painful decline experienced by these non-evangelistic and introverted subcultures. Pain is a major motivator for change, but churches are better off learning from other's mistakes and avoiding the experience. Bruce A. Greer, after relating the struggling pilgrimage of three mainline denominations, tells of their 180-degree turn:

> Yet, the "E word" (evangelism), an anathema for some people in these three traditions, has undeniably found its way to center stage. People at every level of these denominations are talking and learning about a concept and practice that was for many years left to evangelicals and fundamentalists. The word is being reclaimed for mainline Protestant parlance, and the concept is being reconsidered for mainline Protestant praxis. This could not have happened had there not been a concerted effort over the past fifteen years to reclaim personal evangelism, reaffirm new church development, and introduce church growth methodologies[8]

Denominational executives are aware that a nongrowth and introverted subculture can change. On the local level, the single greatest determinant of a growth personality comes from the gradual influence of key leaders. They are ministers, elders, or members who have successfully promoted agendas that were integrated into the corporate life of the church. Past leaders, through their influence, helped to create a church's identity. Likewise, present leaders can use their influence to bolster or change an existing identity. Chapter 3 offers suggestions for leadership attitudes and actions that can help begin the change process.

Responses to Community Conditions

Community churches have gone the way of wide ties and bell-bottom pants. The only difference is that wide ties may come back into fashion (I really hope not), but there is little chance that churches serving an immediate community next to the facilities will return. What we have today are churches serving a ministry radius around the building. About a twenty-minute drive in any direction from the building will compose a church's ministry area.

From a review of the church's membership list, leaders will likely discover that on average about 36% of their church members live within three miles of the building and 41% live between four and nine miles from the facility. A significant difference appeared between members in growing and declining churches. Growing congregations attract members from a greater distance; on the average 28% of their members drive ten or more miles compared to only 17% for declining churches. Regardless, both groups are serving a ministry radius and not an immediate community.

While churches no longer serve a neighborhood, research findings have clearly established the influence of community conditions on membership trends.[9] Church growth specialists have consistently analyzed the local contextual factors for determining realistic church growth potential. Their general conclusion has been that churches are not entirely at the mercy of their ministry radius for growth—they do have choices. If the area is not growing, church growth is still possible through harder and more effective work. Even a growing ministry area does not guarantee growth; effective strategies are still necessary. There are, however, a few community conditions that can prevent growth and almost ensure decline.

Changing Community

What happens immediately around the church building and in a church's ministry radius requires regular monitoring and study. Both areas have an impact on a church's future. The best possible scenario exists when the area immediately around the facility is free from deteriorating physical conditions and escalating crime and the general ministry radius is experiencing growth from an influx of young married couples with a similar socioeconomic background to the congregation. The worst possible scenario for most Anglo churches is simply referred to as a "changing community."

Changing communities are characterized by racial, ethnic, and socioeconomic changes. Conditions around the building dramatically change while the church membership goes unchanged and a growing gap develops between members and community residents. The complexity of dealing with this condition has been the number one contributor to the death of churches in North America.

To understand the changing community scenario requires an understanding of an American social phenomenon. Every congregation has, in addition to a subculture, a specific cultural identity. While some diversity may reside in the membership, a dominant racial, ethnic, and socioeconomic make-up remains. Occasionally, churches will demonstrate positive signs of openness to people from other backgrounds, but prospective new members are attracted only if they can identify with the dominant culture in the congregation. Otherwise, new residents are unreceptive to the church. Congregations can change their own receptivity and inclusiveness, but there is little they can do to change the community's lack of receptivity.

The changing community scenario has occurred repeatedly in urban America. As a community begins to age, property values drop, and a socioeconomic transition begins. The residents that attend a nearby church move out to more stable communities. The members then commute back to their home church. As time goes by, these members, a few at a time, place their membership with congregations closer to their new residence. The church in a changing community then begins slowly to lose its original members, transfer growth diminishes as described above, and, as the gap between members and community widens, the church's evangelistic potential is lost. The single greatest threat to the growth of the church in a changing community is the perceived threat of crime. As a community undergoes change, it usually has an increase in the crime rate. The result is often a slow decline that creates confusion, guilt, and discouragement among the members.

Numerous options exist for churches experiencing this often fatal condition.[10] One of the most difficult to accept, but the most likely hope for growth, is relocation. So often, when the idea of relocation is considered, a high level of guilt develops. Members feel that they are abandoning a neighborhood, and they feel guilty based on the obsolete view of a community church. Often, a relocation does not change significantly their ministry radius, but only provides them a better environment for ministering to their members.

Because the local contextual conditions are significant, churches should relocate their facilities on major transportation arteries, not in the middle of a residential area hidden from view and destined for change. Major highways will increase the size of the ministry radius determined by the twenty-minute drive and improve accessibility to more people. Locate in an area free from deteriorating physical conditions and especially escalating crime. And finally, locate near growing communities. New people moving into new

115

residential areas are the most receptive for transfer and evangelistic growth.

Obviously, a church's subculture will affect the choices made by a congregation. Conservative and outward-oriented subcultures will make every effort to overcome negative community conditions, even if it means eventual relocation. On the other hand, inward-focused congregations tend to become victims of declining communities and seldom have the confidence to relocate to a better contextual setting.

Study Findings

Community conditions were carefully evaluated for each church in the sample. Correlations were conducted between growth and community population changes and ethnic transitions for a three-mile and a ten-mile radius around the churches' facilities. Also included were comparisons of education and income levels between congregations and their communities. Each variable produced only a weak relationship with growth. (See Table A.3 for the results.)

These findings do not nullify the significance of local contextual factors or suggest that leaders can disregard community conditions in their ministry radius. Sample selection in this study partially accounts for the weak relationship between community variables and growth. None of the congregations selected was a newly planted church that usually experiences rapid growth, and only two churches were in changing communities. Of these two, one was experiencing the typical numerical decline and the other was actually growing due to extraordinary ministry efforts. For the most part, each sample had local contextual factors that were similar and stable. Other recent research has noted that communities in general are more stable than ten years ago and, consequently, the local context has declined in explanatory power.[11]

A variable can surface as a significant predictor only if the sample is experiencing a particular condition or exercising a ministry discipline. When a variable produces a statistically significant correlation with growth, then one can have confidence that the variable has a relationship to growth. On the other hand, if the variable is not an existing condition or an effective discipline among the sample, then the lack of strong statistical support does not eliminate the variable as a potential correlate of growth. For example, in this study, membership involvement levels produced only a moderate correlation and community factors produced a weak correlation with growth. Some research and observations done by others, however, have found them as growth predictors.

Another possible reason for the weak correlation is due to a moderately high institutional strength among Churches of Christ. While members do show symptoms of a baby boomer shopping mentality, it is mild compared to membership trends in mainline Protestant denominations and most research establishing the explanatory strength of local contextual factors comes from these groups. Members, even young adults, in Churches of Christ are willing to traverse community boundaries and enter less than ideal conditions to attend a congregation identified with their tradition.

Conclusion

C. Kirk Hadaway, after considering the most recent research insights and surveying the mainline liberal denominations' change efforts, sadly concludes that "mainline denominations retain few visible characteristics that suggest a future growth."[12] They have moved so far from an outward orientation that their situation may be beyond help. *To the contrary, Churches of Christ have a potentially bright future.* Even the declining congregations have not moved beyond the ability to change. Findings clearly reveal that members want their congregations to grow, and they stand poised and ready to follow prepared leadership. Equally important, a conservative subculture is in place for most churches and minimal changes are necessary to develop outward-oriented congregations.

Research findings presented in earlier chapters offer clear choices for churches. More than forty variables surfaced as predictors of growth. Four, in particular, represent major choices for ministry priorities: (1) the ability of the worship assembly to attract new members, (2) adequate staffing ratios, (3) using an evangelistic method that produces results, and (4) having enough groups to attract and assimilate new members. One theme, however, ties all four variables together; growing churches are designing ministry in these four areas to reach young adults in the 20-39 age range.

In part, many of these findings have been presented and positively received by a large number of church members. There appears a readiness among members to implement the changes needed for growth. My prayer is that the research and insights in this book along with membership readiness will encourage leaders to evaluate their existing ministries, build a growth vision, and establish plans and goals for the future.

Appendix A

Pearson Correlations

A description of the data source for this study is presented in the Introduction. As explained, 189 (church-produced) variables were *correlated* with changes in average annual assembly attendance (growth or decline) for a ten-year period.

Correlations measure the linear relationship between two or more conditions or factors (variables). Any study sample must have at least two sets of observed values for computing a correlation. As one set of data increases, does the other set increase or decrease? For example, when churches increase the number of paid staff per 100 members, will their growth trend show an increase or decrease? Correlations provide insight into their relationships.

The data was used to calculate Pearson correlation coefficients (r). A correlation coefficient is an objective way of expressing the relationship between the two variables. Its value ranges from -1.0 to +1.0. The closer the value of the coefficient is to -1.0 or +1.0, the stronger the relationship. Values of -1.0 and +1.0 indicate a perfect linear relationship while zero indicates no relationship. Thus, a coefficient of .50

would reveal a stronger positive relationship than .20; and a coefficient of -.50 would indicate a stronger negative (inverse) relationship than -.20.

When comparing results from different studies, correlation coefficients from each study having the same value are not necessarily equal. To interpret the strength of correlation coefficients, it is helpful to consider their *significance levels*. Researchers commonly use the .05 level of significance as the arbitrary breakpoint between differences due to chance effects. A coefficient that is significant at the .05 level would occur less than 5% of the time due to chance. Therefore, the smaller the value (.01 or .001), the greater the level of significance and less the likelihood it was a chance occurrence. For example, in **Table A.1** the staff-to-member ratio produced a strong correlation coefficient of .51 with a significance level of .001. This means that there is a strong relationship between church growth and more staff per 100 members. And the odds are 1 in 1,000 that the finding was an accidental occurrence.

Another important observation: correlations do not establish causation. In some cases, correlations do involve causation and in other cases they do not. A significant correlation does reveal a linear relationship between the variables and indicates the extent that one variable can be used to predict another variable. The criterion for determining causality should be determined by the nature of the two variables.

Tables A.1, A.2, and A.3 list the significant correlations at the .05 level or greater. A few other variables listed are at or near the .10 level, and some variables are given for comparison purposes that are not statistically significant (ns).

The most manageable variables for researchers are the local contextual factors and local institutional factors. Recent empirical studies modify the institutional factors into two categories: institutional actions (what a church does) and institutional character (what a church is). The same categories are used in grouping variables in this study.

Table A.1 gives the findings for institutional variables (what a church does); **Table A.2** gives the findings for congregational characteristics (what a church is); and **Table A.3** lists the local contextual variables (community setting).

TABLE A.1
Institutional Variables

	Pearson's r	Significance Levels
1. Staff-to-Membership Ratio	.51	.001
2. Elder-to-Membership Ratio	.003	ns
3. Baptisms-to-Membership Ratio	.52	.001
4. Baptisms of Unchurched	.43	.01
5. Groups-to-Membership Ratio	.44	.01
6. % of Member Involvement	.09	ns
7. % of Worship Assembly in Sunday School	.29	.08
8. % of Annual Member Gains	.71	.0001
9. % of Annual Member Losses	.43	.01

Evaluations From Membership Surveys

10. Church Atmosphere Attracts New Members	.43	.01
11. Church is Exciting vs. Dull	.47	.01
12. Church is Active vs. Inactive	.34	.05
13. Church is Creative vs. Unimaginative	.35	.05
14. Church is Free of Troubles vs. Troubled	.39	.01
15. Church Accepts Others vs. Narrow and Critical	.50	.001
16. Church is Well Organized vs. Disorganized	.33	.05
17. Church Sets Goals vs. Accept Things	.30	.07
18. Church Has Excellent Growth Potential	.36	.05
19. Satisfied with Morning Worship Assembly	.34	.05
20. Satisfied with Singing	.30	.07
21. Satisfied with P.M. Worship	.19	ns
22. Satisfied with Mid-week Meeting	.19	ns
23. Look Forward to Morning Worship Assembly	.34	.05
24. Church is Warm and Friendly	.33	.05
25. Visitors Feel Church is Warm and Friendly	.37	.05
26. Preaching Attracts New Members	.34	.05
27. Became Member Because of Worship Assembly	.38	.05

TABLE A.2
Congregational Characteristics

	Pearson's r	Significance Levels
1. Age of Church	-.14	ns
2. Age of Auditorium	-.19	ns

Age Distribution of Members and Children

	Pearson's r	Significance Levels
3. Pre-teens	.30	.07
4. Teens	-.05	ns
5. Age 20-29	.45	.01
6. Age 30-39	.27	.11
7. Age 40-49	-.20	ns
8. Age 50-64	-.44	.01
9. Over 65-	.36	.05

Marital and Parental Status

	Pearson's r	Significance Levels
10. Single	.08	ns
11. Married	.12	ns
12. Children - 0	-.45	.01
13. Children - 1	.09	ns
14. Children - 2	.45	.01
15. Children's Age 0-5	.28	.10
16. Children's Age 6-11	.40	.01

Occupation

	Pearson's r	Significance Levels
17. Professional	.22	ns
18. Clerical	.20	ns
19. Retired	-.43	.01

Other Membership Characteristics

20. Drives 1-3 Miles to Church	-.37	.05
21. Drives 10-15 Miles to Church	.37	.05
22. Attended Less Than 1 Year	.54	.001
23. Attended 1-5 Years	.53	.001
24. Attended 10-19 Years	-.37	.05
25. Attended 20+ Years	-.51	.001
26. Own Home	-.42	.01
27. Rent	.27	.11
28. Single Family House	-.47	.01
29. Apartment or Condo	.54	.001
30. Lived in Community Less Than 1 Year	.47	.01
31. Lived in Community 1-5 Years	.41	.01
32. Lived in Community 6-9 Years	.35	.05
33. Lived in Community 20+ Years	-.53	.001
34. Will Move in 1 Year	.35	.05

Community and Congregational Comparison

35. Age 20-39	.41	.01
36. Age 50 up	-.34	.05

TABLE A.3
Contextual Variables

	Pearson's r	Significance Levels
1. Community Growth (3-Mile Radius)	.02	ns
2. Community Growth (10-Mile Radius)	-.09	ns
3. Ethnic Changes (3-Mile Radius)	-.08	ns
4. Ethnic Changes (10-Mile Radius)	.05	ns
5. Community Education Level (10-Mile Radius)	.20	ns
6. Community Income Level (10-Mile Radius)	-.04	ns

Appendix B

Multiple Regression Analysis

Researchers and analysts readily acknowledge that church growth is due to a large number of complex interrelated factors. This is evident from reviewing the long list of variables given in Appendix A, which is comparable to other studies. Also, many of these factors are measuring the same areas; so how can we determine which variables are clearly the strongest in predictive efficacy? *Multiple regression analysis* provides the tool to discover the variables that are the strongest predictors of church growth.

Multiple regression analysis was applied separately to significant variables related to institutional variables, congregational characteristics, and contextual variables. **Table B.1** lists the four institutional variables that together provided the strongest predictive power for growth. Regression analysis produces a standardized beta value that prioritizes the variables according to predictive power in a multivariate context. They are given in the order of significance determined by beta values, and each variable is discussed in a related chapter.

Regression models produce an adjusted R^2 value (with a maximum value of 1). It reveals what portion of the variance in growth is explained by each group of variables. Institutional factors (what a church does) in **Table B.1** have an adjusted R^2 value of .55, which means they explain 55% of church growth (church attendance change). Local institutional factors in this study prove to be the most powerful predictor of a church's future.

TABLE B.1
Multiple Regression: Institutional Variables

	Pearson's r	Standardized Beta
1. Became Member Because of Worship Assembly	.34	.43
2. Staff-to-Membership Ratio	.51	.39
3. Baptisms-to-Membership Ratio	.52	.24
4. Groups-to- Membership Ratio	.44	.21
Adjusted R^2 = .55		

Table B.2 lists the three variables that produce the greatest predictive power among congregational characteristics. Each factor describes key demographic characteristics in the church. Chapter 2 discusses these key variables along with an important appeal for age balance in churches. Congregational characteristics explain 37% of church growth. This is a close second to institutional variables and this set is interrelated with church activities. Church demographics affect church programs, and over time church programs affect church demographics.

TABLE B.2
Multiple Regression: Congregational Characteristics

	Pearson's r	Standardized Beta
1. Age 20-29	.45	.36
2. Children - 2	.45	.36
3. Age 50-64	-.44	-.22
Adjusted R^2 = .37		

None of the local contextual factors in this study proved statistically significant as a predictor of growth. An assessment of these findings is given in Chapter 7. The evidence from case studies and research affirms the importance of community conditions on growth; so further efforts were made to discover the impact of community factors.

An untested theory states that church growth is more dependent upon community mobility than community growth. A community may have a highly mobile population and yet register no net growth. The closest way to test this theory with the available data was to compare the mobility of church members with church growth. This has limitations from the fact that it is possible to have stable (nonmobile) members in a mobile community, but it is unlikely to have mobile members in a stable community. Community conditions do affect the church's membership characteristics, and membership mobility, like other community factors, is beyond the church's control.

Table B.3 lists two variables, reflecting community mobility, that explain 27% of the variance. Even with the limitation, it appears that community mobility does relate to church growth. Certainly, further study is needed to test this theory.

TABLE B.3
Multiple Regression: Contextual Variables

	Pearson's r	Standardized Beta
1. Live in Community Less Than 1 Year	.47	.44
2. Will Move in 1 Year	.35	.30
Adjusted R^2 = .27		

Appendix C

Other resources from the Center for Church Growth:

Church Services
- Individualized Congregational Church Growth Workshop
- Diagnostic Evaluation
- Diagnostic Follow-up Evaluation
- Managing Home Groups for Growth
- Growing the Church Through the Bible Class Program
- Leadership and Team Building Workshop

Magazine
- *Church Growth Magazine* is published quarterly, and its goal is to provide effective and practical ideas to church leaders and members.

Book
- *Church Growth Through Groups: Strategies for Varying Levels of Christian Community.* Center for Church Growth, 1990.

For additional information on these services and resources, contact:

Center for Church Growth
P. O. Box 691006
Houston, Texas 77269-1006
(713) 894-4391

HELP YOUR MEMBERS CATCH A VISION WITH . . .

 **Magazine**

Every page filled with great ideas to inspire leaders and members. Each quarterly issue offers
- Examples of growing congregations
- Practical ideas to increase membership
- New methods for outreach and growth
- The latest research and trends in growing churches

----------------------------------Clip and Mail Today----------------------------------

Notes

Introduction

1. George Barna, *Today's Pastor* (Ventura, CA: Regal Books, 1993), p. 46.

2. John W. Ellas, *Church Growth Through Groups*. Can be purchased from the Center for Church Growth, P. O. Box 691006, Houston, TX 77269-1006, (713) 894-4391.

3. Martin E. Marty, "Forward," *Understanding Church Growth and Decline: 1950-1978*, ed. Dean R. Hoge and David A. Roozen (New York: Pilgrim Press, 1979), p. 10.

4. C. Kirk Hadaway and David A. Roozen, "Denominational Growth and Decline," *Church and Denominational Growth*, ed. David A. Roozen and C. Kirk Hadaway (Nashville: Abingdon Press, 1993), pp. 41-42.

5. James D. Hunter, *Evangelism: The Coming Generation* (Chicago: University of Chicago Press, 1987), p. 203.

6. Dean R. Hoge, "A Test of Theories of Denominational Growth and Decline," *Understanding Church Growth and Decline: 1950-1978*, p. 190.

7. David A. Roozen and Jackson W. Carroll, "Recent Trends in Church Membership and Participation: An Introduction," *Understanding Church Growth and Decline: 1950-1978*, pp. 39-40.

8. Michael J. Donahue and Peter L. Benson, "Belief Style, Congregational Climate, and Program Quality," *Church and Denominational Growth*, p. 231.

9. Daniel V. A. Olson, "Congregational Growth and Decline in Indiana Among Five Mainline Denominations," *Church and Denominational Growth*, p. 219.

10. Roozen and Carroll, "Recent Trends," pp. 28-32.

11. It is also referred to as an incidental sample. See J.P. Guilfort and Benjamin Fruchter, *Fundamental Statistics in Psychology and Education* 6th ed. (New York: McGraw-Hill, 1978), p. 123.

Chapter One
Generations in Conflict

1. This material was adapted from an article I submitted to the *Church Growth Journal of the North American Society for Church Growth*. A special thanks to editor John N. Vaughan for permission to present it here.

2. Sociologists divide the generational periods in different ways with multiple groupings for both pre- and post-war generations. Even though there is more than one pre-war generation, I will at times refer to the pre- or post-war generation as a single group.

3. Wade Clark Roof, *A Generation of Seekers: The Spiritual Journeys of the Baby Boom Generation* (New York: HarperCollins, 1993), pp. 56-57.

4. Edward E. Plowman, *National and International Religion Report* 5, no. 11 (20 May 1991): 8.

5. Richard Vara, "Ministers Up In Air Over Firings," *Houston Chronicle*, 8 May 1993, p. 1 (E).

6. George H. Gallup, Jr., "Worship," *Religion in America 1992-1993*, ed. Robert Bezilla (Princeton, NJ: The Princeton Religion Research Center, 1993), p. 43.

7. Ibid.

8. Roof, *A Generation of Seekers*, p. 272.

9. Ken Dychtwald and Joe Flower, *Age Wave: The Challenges and Opportunities of an Aging America* (Los Angeles: Jeremy P. Tarcher, 1989), p. xix.

10. Ibid., p. 13.

11. David A. Roozen and C. Kirk Hadaway, "Individuals and the Church Choice," *Church and Denominational Growth*, p. 241.

12. Ibid., p. 242.

13. For a scholarly treatment of this text, see Kenneth V. Neller, "I Corinthians 9:19-23: A Model for Those Who Seek to Win Souls," *Restoration Quarterly* 29 (3): 129-142.

14. In addition to the books already noted, I highly recommend these: Leith Anderson, *Dying For Change* (Minneapolis: Bethany Book

Publishers, 1990); Robert L. Blast, *The Missing Generation* (Monrovia, CA: Church Growth, Inc., 1991); Robert T. Gribbon, *Developing Faith in Young Adults* (Washington, DC: The Alban Institute, 1990); and Doug Murren, *The Baby Boomerang* (Ventura, CA: Regal Books, 1990).

15. Roof, *A Generation of Seekers*, p. 3.

16. Gallup, *Religion in America*, p. 3.

17. Cynthia W. Sayre and Herb Miller, *The Christian Church (Disciples of Christ) New Member Study*, Department of Evangelism and Membership of the Division of Homeland Ministries of the Christian Church (Disciples of Christ), (Indianapolis: 1985), p. 16.

Chapter Two
Neglecting a Generation

1. Win Arn and Charles Arn, "Riding the Wave of Silver and Gray," *Leadership* 11(4):112.

2. U.S. Bureau of the Census, *Statistical Abstract of the United States: 1992* (Washington, DC: U.S. Government Printing Office, 1992), p. 15.

3. Olson, "Congregational Growth," p. 217-218.

4. George H. Gallup, Jr., "Additional Observations and Recommendations," *The Unchurched American—10 Years Later* (Princeton, NJ: The Princeton Religion Research Center, 1988), p. 11.

5. Robert T. Gribbon, *Developing Faith in Young Adults: Effective Ministry with 18-35 Year Olds* (Washington, DC: The Alban Institute, 1990), p. 38.

6. David M. Malone, "Assessing Patterns of Disengagement and Re-Entry Into Local Congregations of Churches of Christ" (D.Min. thesis, Abilene Christian University, 1992), pp. 169-171.

7. Roof, *A Generation of Seekers*, p. 155.

8. Ibid.

9. Ibid., p. 212.

Chapter Three
Leadership Choices

1. Richard Saul Wurman, *Information Anxiety* (New York: Bantam Books, 1989), p. 32.
2. Ibid., p. 36.
3. Win Arn, *The Church Growth Ratio Book* (Pasadena, CA: Church Growth, Inc., 1987), p. 16.
4. Ibid., p. 17.
5. Data for the graphs are based on the 1992 *Church Compensation Report* (Carol Stream, IL: Christianity Today, Inc., 1991). John C. LaRue, Jr., research director for CT, provided the Center for Church Growth the figures for graph one. The other two graphs were presented in *Your Church* 39, no. 6 (Nov./Dec., 1993): 48. Used by permission.
6. For a complete description of the 200 barrier, see Ellas, *Church Growth Through Groups.*
7. Carl George, *How to Break Growth Barriers* (Grand Rapids: Baker Books, 1993).
8. C. Kirk Hadaway, *Growing Off the Plateau: A Summary of the 1988 "Church on the Plateau" Survey.* (Nashville: Sunday School Board of the Southern Baptist Convention, 1989).
9. C. Kirk Hadaway, *Church Growth Principles: Separating Fact from Fiction* (Nashville: Broadman, 1991), pp. 162-166.
10. Ibid., p. 103.
11. Hadaway, *Growing Off the Plateau,* p. 8.
12. Ibid., p. 10.

Chapter Four
Worship Choices

1. For an introduction to worship resources, see *Wineskins* 1, no. 5 (September, 1992).
2. Hadaway, *Growing Off the Plateau,* p. 20.
3. Ibid.

4. Ronald Allen and Gordon Borror, *Worship: Rediscovering the Missing Jewel* (Portland: Multnomah Press, 1982), pp. 77-89.

5. Ibid., p. 19.

6. Everett Ferguson, *Early Christians Speak* (Austin, TX: Sweet Publishing, 1971), pp. 72-73.

7. Ralph P. Martin, *The Worship of God* (Grand Rapids: Wm. B. Eerdmans, 1982), p. 215.

8. Herb Miller, *How to Build a Magnetic Church* (Nashville: Abingdon Press, 1987), p. 51.

9. Danny McKinney, "A Survey: Religious Attitudes of Young Adults," *Church Growth* 9 (3): 3.

10. F. LaGard Smith, *The Cultural Church* (Nashville: 20th Century Christian, 1992), p. 48.

11. James Emery White, *Opening the Front Door: Worship and Church Growth* (Nashville: Convention Press, 1992), p. 69.

12. McKinney, "A Survey," p. 3.

13. For a history of words and sentences, see Rudolf Flesch, *The Art of Readable Writing* (New York: Macmillan Publishing, 1962).

14. Evertt W. Huffard, "Leading Growing Churches: The Role of the Preacher," *Church Growth* 9 (2): 7.

15. Roy M. Oswald and Speed B. Leas, *The Inviting Church: A Study of New Member Assimilation* (Washington, DC: The Alban Institute, 1987), p. 26.

16. Hadaway, *Church Growth Principles,* p. 90.

17. Hadaway, *Growing Off the Plateau,* p. 5.

18. White, *Opening the Front Door,* p. 82.

19. Ibid., p. 84.

20. Ibid., p. 83.

Chapter Five
Involvement Choices

1. Arn, *The Church Growth Ratio Book,* p. 25.

2. Olson, "Congregational Growth," p. 221.

3. Hadaway, *Growing Off the Plateau,* p. 19.

4. For specific help with resources, contact the Center for Church Growth, P. O. Box 691006, Houston, TX 77269-1006, or call (713) 894-4391.

5. Roger E. Hedlund, *The Mission of the Church in the World* (Grand Rapids: Baker Book House, 1985), p. 259.

6. Donahue and Benson, "Belief Style, " p. 239.

7. George, *Prepare Your Church for the Future,* (Tarrytown, NY: Revell Co., 1991), p. 101.

8. Hadaway, *Growing Off the Plateau,* p. 18.

9. Arn, *The Church Growth Ratio Book,* p. 31.

10. Flavil R. Yeakley, Jr., *Why Churches Grow* (Broken Arrow, OK: Christian Communications, Inc., 1979), p. 41.

11. Ibid., pp. 42-45.

12. *Worker Analysis* (Pasadena, CA: Charles E. Fuller Institute, 1981).

Chapter Six
Outreach Choices

1. For example, see Roger E. Hedlund, *The Mission of the Church in the World* (Grand Rapids: Baker Book House, 1991); George W. Peters, *A Theology of Church Growth* (Grand Rapids: Zondervan, 1981); and Charles E. Van Engen, *The Growth of the True Church* (Amsterdam: Rodopi, 1981).

2. C. Kirk Hadaway and David A. Roozen, "The Growth and Decline of Congregations," *Church and Denominational Growth,* p. 129.

3. George G. Hunter, III, *To Spread the Power: Church Growth in the Wesleyan Spirit* (Nashville: Abingdon, 1987), p. 100.

4. Ibid., pp. 100-101.

5. Ibid., pp. 105-106.

6. C. Peter Wagner, *Your Church Can Grow: Seven Vital Signs of a Healthy Church* (Glendale: Regal Books, 1976), p. 135.

7. Hadaway, *Growing Off the Plateau,* p. 13.

8. For a list of resources, contact the Center for Church Growth, P. O. Box 691006, Houston, TX 77269-1006, or call (713) 894-4391.

9. Hadaway, *Church Growth Principles,* pp. 79-80.

10. Yeakley, *Why Churches Grow*, p. 9.
11. *Merriam Webster's Collegiate Dictionary*, Tenth Edition, p. 929.
12. Yeakley, *Why Churches Grow*, p. 54.
13. Ibid., p. 64.
14. Ibid., p. 59.
15. Ibid., p. 63.

Chapter Seven
Identity Choices

1. Bruce A. Greer, "Strategies for Evangelism and Growth in Three Denominations (1965-1990)," *Church and Denominational Growth*, p. 108.
2. Dean M. Kelly, "Commentary: Is Religion a Dependent Variable?" *Understanding Church Growth and Decline: 1950-78*, pp. 336-337.
3. Oswald and Leas, *The Inviting Church*, p. 47.
4. Ibid., p. 48.
5. Greer, "Strategies," pp. 87-111.
6. Ibid., p. 89.
7. Herb Miller, "Is It All in Your Mind," *Net Results* 13, no. 6 (January, 1992): 3-6.
8. Greer, "Strategies," p. 110.
9. Studies presented in *Church and Denominational Growth, Church Growth Principles,* and *Growing Off the Plateau* offer clear evidence that community conditions affect church growth.
10. For other viable options, see Evertt W. Huffard, "Churches in Ethnic Transition," *Perspectives on World Evangelism*, ed. C. Philip Slate (Searcy, AR: Resource Publications, 1988), pp. 161-183.
11. Olson, "Congregational Growth," p. 215.
12. C. Kirk Hadaway, "Church Growth in North America," *Church and Denominational Growth*, p. 350.

Selected Bibliography

Allen, Ronald, and Gordon Borror. *Worship: Rediscovering the Missing Jewel*. Portland: Multnomah Press, 1982.

Anderson, Leith. *Dying for Change*. Minneapolis: Bethany Book Publishers, 1990.

Anderson, Ray S. *Minding God's Business*. Grand Rapids: Wm. B. Eerdmans, 1986.

_____, ed. *Theological Foundations for Ministry*. Grand Rapids: Wm. B. Eerdmans, 1979.

Arn, Win. *The Church Growth Ratio Book*. Pasadena, CA: Church Growth, Inc., 1987.

Arn, Win, and Charles Arn. *The Master's Plan for Making Disciples*. Pasadena, CA: Church Growth, Inc., 1979.

Arn, Win, Carrol Nyquist, and Charles Arn. *Who Cares About Love?* Pasadena, CA: Church Growth, Inc., 1986.

Banks, Robert. *Paul's Idea of Community: The Early House Churches in their Historical Setting*. Grand Rapids: Wm. B. Eerdmans, 1980.

Beasley-Murray, Paul, and Alan Wilkinson. *Turning the Tide: An Assessment of Baptist Church Growth in England*. London, England: British Bible, 1981.

Blast, Robert L. *The Missing Generation*. Monrovia, CA: Church Growth, Inc., 1991.

Dale, Robert D. *To Dream Again*. Nashville: Broadman, 1981.

Dychtwald, Ken, and Joe Fowler. *Age Wave: The Challenges and Opportunities of an Aging America*. Los Angeles: Jeremy P. Tarcher, Inc., 1989.

Ellas, John W. *Church Growth Through Groups: Strategies for Varying Levels of Christian Community*. Houston: Center for Church Growth, 1990.

Ferguson, Everett. *Early Christians Speak*. Austin, TX: Sweet Publishing, 1971.

George, Carl F. *Prepare Your Church for the Future*. Tarrytown, NY: Revell, 1991.

George, Carl F. and Robert E. Logan. *Leading and Managing Your Church*. Old Tappan, NJ: Revell, 1987.

Gribbon, Robert T. *Developing Faith in Young Adults: Effective Ministry with 18-35 Year Olds*. Washington, DC: The Alban Institute, 1990.

Hadaway, C. Kirk. *Church Growth Principles: Separating Fact from Fiction*. Nashville: Broadman, 1991.

_____. *Growing Off the Plateau: A Summary of the 1988 "Church on the Plateau" Survey*. Nashville: Sunday School Board of the Southern Baptist Convention, 1989.

Hoge, Dean R., and David A. Roozen, eds. *Understanding Church Growth and Decline: 1950-1978*. New York: Pilgrim, 1979.

Hunter, III, George G. *To Spread the Power: Church Growth in the Wesleyan Spirit*. Nashville: Abingdon, 1987.

Keifert, Patrick R. *Welcoming the Stranger: Public Theology of Worship and Evangelism*. Minneapolis: Fortress Press, 1992.

Kelley, Dean M. *Why Conservative Churches Are Growing*. Rev. ed., Macon, GA: Mercer University, 1986.

Logan, Robert E. *Beyond Church Growth*. Old Tappan, NJ: Revell, 1989.

Malherbe, Abraham J. *Social Aspects of Early Christianity*. Minneapolis: Fortress Press, 1983.

McGavran, Donald A. *Effective Evangelism: A Theological Mandate*. Phillipsburg, NJ: Presbyterian and Reformed, 1988.

Meeks, Wayne A. *The First Urban Christians*. New Haven, CT: Yale University Press, 1983.

Miller, Herb. *How to Build a Magnetic Church*. Nashville: Abingdon, 1987.

Murren, Doug. *The Baby Boomerang*. Ventura, CA: Regal, 1990.

Oswald, Roy M. and Speed B. Leas. *The Inviting Church: A Study of New Members Assimilation*. Washington, DC: The Alban Institute, 1987.

Peters, George W. *A Theology of Church Growth*. Grand Rapids: Zondervan, 1981.

Poloma, Margaret M. and George H. Gallup, Jr. *Varieties of Prayer: A Survey Report*. Philadelphia: Trinity Press International, 1991.

BIBLIOGRAPHY

Rainer, Thom S. *The Book of Church Growth: History, Theology, and Principles.* Nashville: Broadman, 1993.

Roof, Wade Clark. *A Generation of Seekers: The Spiritual Journeys of the Baby Boom Generation.* San Francisco: Harper Collins, 1993.

Roozen, David A., and C. Kirk Hadaway, eds. *Church and Denominational Growth.* Nashville: Abingdon, 1993.

Smith, F. LaGard. *The Cultural Church.* Nashville: 20th Century Christian, 1992.

Tippett, Alan R. *Church Growth and the Word of God: The Biblical Basis of the Church Growth Viewpoint.* Grand Rapids: Wm. B. Eerdmans, 1970.

Vaughan, John N. *The Large Church: A Twentieth Century Expression of the First Century Church.* Grand Rapids: Baker, 1985.

Wagner, C. Peter. *Church Growth and the Whole Gospel: A Biblical Mandate.* San Francisco: Harper & Row, 1981.

_____. *Leading Your Church to Growth.* Ventura, CA: Regal, 1984.

_____. *Our Kind of People: The Ethical Dimensions of Church Growth in America.* Atlanta: John Knox, 1979.

_____. *Your Church Can Be Healthy.* Nashville: Abingdon, 1979.

_____. *Your Church Can Grow: Seven Vital Signs of a Healthy Church.* Glendale, CA: Regal Books, 1976.

White, James Emery, *Opening the Front Door: Worship and Church Growth.* Nashville: Convention Press, 1992.

Wilkie, Richard B. *And Are We Yet Alive?* Nashville: Abingdon, 1986.

Yeakley, Flavil R., Jr. *Why Churches Grow.* Broken Arrow, OK: Christian Communications, 1979.

Index

INDEX

-W-

Wagner, C. Peter, 100, 138, 143
Well-organized, 49, 80
White, James Emery, 71, 137, 143
World War II, 2-3, 13, 19
Worship Assemblies, 59, 104
    celebration, 61-64
    climate, 60, 65-67, 71, 133
    excellence, 32, 42, 63-64
    exciting, 60, 71-72, 106
    joyful, 60-62, 71
    meditative, 60
    members' evaluation of, 58-59
    planning, 53

predictability, 64
relaxed, 60
reverence, 62
singing, 59, 71
style, 8, 59, 72, 133, 138
variety, 63-64, 71
warm and friendly, 21, 32, 42-
    43, 65-66, 71-72
Wurman, Richard, 37, 136

-Y-

Yeakley, Jr., Flavil, xvi, 88, 103,
    105, 138-139, 143